Tschanna Taylor

H.E.R. Extreme Makeover
Reflections of Healing, Equipping, and Restoring Messes to Masterpieces

Compiled By:
Tschanna Taylor

Forewords By:
Nanette Floyd Patterson
Felecia Killings

H.E.R. Poem By:
Annie Davis Lee

Contributions By (in alphabetical order):
Alisa Green
Angela Chance
Cheryl Menifee
Christina Saunders
Erin Fuller-Russell
Kier Ayers
Nakisha Blackwell
Shanae Starnes
Sharice Rush
Tina Moore

Pearly Gates Publishing LLC
INSPIRING CHRISTIAN AUTHORS TO BE AUTHORS

Pearly Gates Publishing, LLC, Houston, Texas (USA)

H.E.R. Extreme Makeover
Reflections of Healing, Equipping, and Restoring Messes to Masterpieces

Copyright © 2019
Tschanna Taylor

All Rights Reserved.
No portion of this publication may be reproduced, stored in any electronic system, or transmitted in any form or by any means (electronic, mechanical, photocopy, recording, or otherwise) without written permission from the author or publisher. Brief quotations may be used in literary reviews.

ISBN 13: 978-1-947445-56-7
Library of Congress Control Number: 2019938200

Some names and identifying details have been changed to protect the privacy of individuals.

Scripture references are used with permission from Zondervan via Biblegateway.com.
Public Domain.

For information and bulk ordering, contact:
Pearly Gates Publishing, LLC
Angela Edwards, CEO
P.O. Box 62287
Houston, TX 77205
BestSeller@PearlyGatesPublishing.com

Dedication

This book is dedicated to **YOU** if:

You've ever been emotionally scarred, harbor deep, unspeakable pain, and are defined by harsh criticism, exclusion, or rejection, which grips you like a chokehold.

Be **HEALED, EQUIPPED,** and **RESTORED** today as you wade and reflect through the pages of this book. Begin to change as you embrace your truth—no matter what hardships you have suffered…no matter how many people or circumstances have tried to make you think you have no value.

Although you may not understand or even like the process you are in, trust the Master Designer! Be assured He is working to redefine and rebuild you into a beautiful masterpiece so that you, too, can share your story with others.

Here's to your **HEALING** and **RESTORATION**!

~ *Tschanna Taylor* ~

""For I know the plans I have for you," declares the LORD, "plans to prosper you and not to harm you, plans to give you hope and a future.""
Jeremiah 29:11, NIV

Acknowledgements

Writing this book has been both a humbling and healing experience for me. Too many times, I would shrink back, fearing success due to old, limited beliefs. Now, I share my story boldly, confidently, unashamedly, and unapologetically.

First and foremost, I want to thank **God** for being the epitome of everything I need, for the guidance in the process of writing this book, and for His grace and mercy in the process of my very being and my life.

Thank you to my **Husband** who always knows what to say and was a perfect support of encouragement and motivation during the whole process of writing and, most especially, in the growth of my life and business.

Thank you to my **Son** for being so patient, coming along for the ride, and taking your own notes and applying them when you have a moment in your own business. Mommy is forever grateful for you, son.

Thank you to my publisher and SisterFriend, **Angela Edwards**, and the Pearly Gates Publishing staff. It was from the first book collaboration with LaDeema Burns that captivated me and prompted the desire to work with you. You have helped to take the vision and we've made it plain! Thank you for your heart and the help that you are.

Thank you to the **Co-Authors** who readily said "YES!" and for trusting me from when we first got started in January 2018 until today. You took copious notes and listened. Now, I'm so happy to see the fruits of your labor because you are applying what you were taught. What I've learned from all of you this past year is that teaching is not about "information"; it's about having an honest, intellectual relationship with your students. Infinitely, my prayer for you is that the lessons I shared never stop encouraging you to explore every possibility afforded to you and that you never miss any opportunities that come your way.

Thank you to all of my Mentors, Coaches, and Spiritual Advisors who have been active in supporting me and my life's endeavors. Most especially, I am appreciative of **Evangelist Annie R. Davis-Lee**, who has been instrumental in showing me my own strength and helping me to see the conviction of my heart and significance of life's purpose.

To **Master IIIScoach Nanette Floyd Patterson**, who introduced me to the coaching industry, how to ask a lot of questions, W.I.G.S. (What Is God Saying to you), and laying the unnecessary extra "stuff" to rest.

To **Felecia Killings**, you listened! You didn't judge. You shared with me how to be authentic and unapologetic in sharing my truths as well as learning how to scale my business and ministry seamlessly.

To **Elder Nicole S. Mason, Esq.**, you taught me to show up great! You provided a safe space for me with women who allowed me to let my hair down and not ever worry if it would be plastered all over social media. Even under pressure, you taught me to continually keep praising and worshipping God because my greatest blessing is beyond my comfort zone.

To **Pastor Ida Roundtree**, thank you for exemplifying the life of a Pastor. I've taken many spiritual analysis tests and every year, the top three come back as Shepherd, Leadership, and Administration. Over the years, you've shown me a shepherd's heart—one full of grace with a zeal for the gospel.

To **Patricia Rogers Richardson**, thank you for stepping in to represent the Fields family and loving me as if they are still here with us, not skipping a beat.

To **Pastor Julian F. Couch, Jr.**, I thank you for recognizing the gifts within me, allowing me to come to the training ground so that I can take the knowledge out to the masses. You teach me to stand firm with God's Word as the ultimate authority, being bold and confident in the face of adversity.

Thank you to my **Family and Friends** for the love that you show and the support that you give to help me help others.

Last but not least, I thank **YOU**. Yes, YOU! The one who is reading this book. This book would be of no use without YOU. Thank YOU for giving this book life and purpose. From my heart to yours, may YOU be filled with love and wisdom and be empowered to live the life YOU want—with happiness, freedom, healing, equipping, and restoring!

Blessings!

~ Tschanna M. Taylor, MBA ~

Foreword by Nanette Floyd Patterson

Tschanna has woven together 11 women's stories into a healing masterpiece. God has truly blessed her with the gift of writing, which is proven evident by her five Amazon Best-Selling books. In this book, Tschanna gives women a platform of opportunity to embrace what is most feared. As you'll discover after reading this book, healing is a journey. Everyone has their own journey they must travel.

Tschanna uses her thirst for knowledge and truth to help others catapult to their desired destination. I've known Tschanna for more than four years, and her love for helping other women heal and be restored is obvious as soon as she opens her mouth and shares her testimony. She has successfully achieved various certifications and holds an MBA—amongst other formal credentials. She shares on several platforms how women can rebuild their self-confidence and self-worth by sharing their stories.

This masterpiece that Tschanna has orchestrated offers healing and restoration to the woman who believes that healing is far away and may not be for her. This book offers women the opportunity to get to their point of healing and restoration, to reflect, and to see their "messes turned into masterpieces." I'm reminded of a quote by Yoko Ono that says, "Healing yourself is connected with healing others." This book is evidence of that truth.

Tschanna Taylor

~ *Nanette Floyd Patterson*, MA, LPC ~

Christian Counselor & Master HIScoach
The Seed Planter Coaching & Counseling, PLLC
www.the-seed-planter.com
Twitter: @HISentrepreneur
Facebook: NanetteFloydPatterson
YouTube: TheSeedPlanter

Foreword by Felecia S. Killings

Dear Reader,

I want you to think for just a moment about all the pain, all the heartaches, and all the trials you've encountered.

Now, imagine yourself sitting in a room full of women who are delivering similar stories as your own. These women — through their shared lived experiences — find themselves embracing you and your struggles. No judgment. No condemnation. Just pure love.

That is essentially what you will receive as you open the pages of this remarkable and breathtaking anthology, H.E.R. Extreme Makeover. In this resource, Tschanna Taylor introduces eleven women who each give their personal testimonies of how we are, at times, uncertain of our life's purpose. We question why things happen to us the way they do, especially during our childhood years. We look for answers, hoping to find the reasons for why we endured such turmoil. Far too often, we fail to see the powerful lessons that emerge as a result of our hardships.

I first met Tschanna Taylor in 2016 when I launched my online school for Christian Authors, LiyahAmore University. She became a student of mine, and I could sense (even during our coaching sessions) that her testimony and ministry would empower so many other women.

Tschanna Taylor

It's not easy to share some of the painful experiences in a book. It's not easy confessing those things we wish to remain hidden from others, but Tschanna risks it all for the sake of helping others. This work is truly a reflection of her wisdom, her strength, and her ability to change lives.

As you read each story, understand that you, too, contain the power to change a person's life…if you are willing to take your story and transform it into a ministry of deliverance. This book is just the resource that will give you the strength needed to take that leap of faith.

Be blessed, Dear Reader!

And, as always, **let's grow together!**

~ Felecia S. Killings ~

Founder and CEO of FKMinistries
Executive Director of LiyahAmore University and Publishing

Prologue

One of my favorite scriptures is:

"And we know that all that happens to us is working for our good if we love God and are fitting into His plans"
~ Romans 8:28, TLB ~

Just think: Ever since you were small, someone has been telling you what you can't do. Then, as you get older, there are lots of people who not only tell you what you can't do, but also what you can't achieve.

"You're not smart enough."

"You're not in the 'elite' group."

"You can't be a professional cosmetologist."

"There is no way you will ever complete your degree."

Sadly, we accept the words deposited into us for fear of criticism from others. For this reason, even into our adulthood, we're often waiting for someone to tell us it's okay to operate in our God-given purpose. Why? Because we are too afraid that if we blow it, we'll look crazy — and then what will they say?

"I told you that you couldn't do it."

Several years ago, I experienced a difficult situation when I first entered the writing industry. I admit that although

I was a novice, I didn't execute my due diligence by asking more questions, researching, and being confident enough to know that no matter the decision I made, there was always going to be either a lesson or blessing from the experience. I spent hundreds of thousands "investing" in myself, with hopes that someone more successful than me could validate the dreams I had. Ah, yes! Then, things would take off for me the way I dreamt them. Deep down, I didn't want to look like a failure because the truth is this: That conditioned way of thinking started long before I entered into adulthood. It started when I was a child.

One day, I was sitting outside on the bench during my break at work when the Holy Spirit spoke to my heart and said, *"Everything you went through has purpose there! Your feet are anointed to travel the world to share with others this message of hope and restoration!"* If God is for you, who can be against you? (Romans 8:31) His Spirit acknowledged that through all the tests I've had to endure, it was time to heal and move forward into all that He had for me. He showed me the beauty of my "messes" (tests).

So many women needed to know that all things work together for the good of them who love the Lord. It didn't matter how many mistakes we made. Even through our mess, God still loves us and can still be used for His glory! When we go through different trials, we never know what the path that is laid before us will be.

For the first time in my life, I took full responsibility for every decision I made and how I responded to different situations. I no longer blamed my mother, my stepfather, my father, ex-boyfriends, husbands, former bosses, friendships and business partnerships that ended, church hurt, and more. From that moment, God was moving quickly, picking me apart piece-by-piece and rebuilding me into the woman He knew me to be and the woman I am today. I was able to completely let go of all that "mess" I had been holding onto for years. He has removed all my insecurities and enhanced my talent as a writer so that I could do His work. He was just waiting for me to surrender.

H.E.R. Extreme Makeover: Reflections of Healing, Equipping, and Restoring Messes into Masterpieces is not "just a book." It is a movement to help women and men around the world who are hurting.

I have been writing since the 9th grade. Never would I have thought God would lead me in this way. Back then, I used my diary to pen my thoughts. We didn't call them 'journals' then (and no, I am not **THAT** old). 😊 I had to write to release the hurt, pain, and confusion of why things happened the way they did as I worked my way through feeling useless because I couldn't control a single thing as a child. I had a difficult time trusting people because the ones I thought would protect and keep me safe actually ended up being the ones who snatched away that trust. My diary was the way I released it *all*.

I knew that as a woman of God, it was my duty to answer the call and stop running. Oh! And I ran for over 20 years! Baby, I was tired! My story is the story of many women. I wrote this book, along with the co-authors, to remind you that it is not over. God will free you from any bondage that is keeping you from moving forward in your purpose. He has strategically placed each and every one of us on our own path (see Jeremiah 29:11).

This book was written from a Christian perspective, but I truly believe that every woman from every walk of life can benefit from the information it contains. We are ALL God's daughters. Contrary to what others may say, He is waiting for women of all religious backgrounds to come to Him and surrender.

Before I close, I want you to answer the following questions, being completely honest and true to where you are in your life right now. Write them in your journal and date it. When you complete this book, go back and do this exercise again. Feel free to share your results with me by emailing me at messintoamasterpiece@gmail.com and I'll be sure to reply.

- ❖ Who am I?
- ❖ Who do I hope to become?
- ❖ What do I think I will gain from this book?
- ❖ What are the goals I will set for myself to become a better me?
- ❖ When will I start transforming my life?
- ❖ Where in my life will these changes take place?
- ❖ Why do I feel the need to make changes in my life?
- ❖ When do I hope to begin seeing results of this transformation?

It is my hope that as you read this book, you take personal accountability for your life. Pray, meditate, speak God's Word over you and your family, forgive quickly, write in your favorite journal, and have meetings with your Sisterhood, book club, or women's circle so that you can receive the answers you've been seeking—answers that will unleash the true meaning of your purpose.

Remember: Everything you've been through will <u>*never*</u> go to waste. **NEVER!** God can take your "mess" and turn it into a "masterpiece"!

Introduction

As far back as I can remember, women were treated poorly. Reality shows didn't just appear on the scene 10+ years ago; they existed even in the Bible days. Common names such as Eve, Sarah, Rachel, Rahab, Ruth, and Esther are well-known to most of us. There were also women in the Bible who served as unsung heroines whom you didn't hear that much about such as Abigail, Sheerah, Dinah, Hassophereth, and Huldah. These women didn't know anything about Facebook, Instagram, Twitter, or SnapChat. They cooked their foods over an open fire, carried their garbage to the dump, and got their water from the river. Life and death occurred before them and they didn't have drugs to ease their pain. These women knew life without camouflage. They learned about faith by way of their mistakes or their "messes" and the "messes" of others. The Bible tells their stories with such grace, poise, candor, love, understanding, and sympathy.

The Merriam-Webster Dictionary defines the word 'mess' as "disorderly, offensive, or unpleasant because of blundering, negligence, or misconduct." If you had to put a picture to the definition, you would see all of our faces from this book. We all have experienced a "mess" or two in our lives.

In *H.E.R. Extreme Makeover: Reflections of Healing, Equipping, and Restoring Messes to Masterpieces*, the lives of eleven women are on display, offering a fresh perspective on the story of true makeovers. These women have a long and colorful lives. You will 'meet' ministers, teachers, mothers, daughters, business owners, ex-female offenders, abused women, single women, married women, fatherless women…and the list could go on and on.

Far from being one-dimensional, these are real women who struggled with life's challenges daily—some even inadvertently creating self-challenges. Even though our cultures are vastly different, our collective stories are about life, love, knowing your worth, forgiveness, worry for our children, failed relationships, and being bold and confident. What this means is that we all had to experience a process! The process doesn't always feel good, but we can make it through when we heal, obtain the tools necessary to move forward, seek help, and allow for restoration to take place in our lives.

In this book, the authors—through their stories—reveal so much about God's real intention for us all. That intention is concerning God's grace, relentless love, and creative ability to bring good from the most desperate of circumstances.

I challenge you to learn from these great women. Be reminded that we are all precious in God's sight. You may be confused, frustrated, and fear the unknown. Everything that you've been through has a purpose attached to it. No need to worry! God is putting together a comeback for you! Your "mess" will be turned into a "masterpiece"!

If you remember nothing else shared on the pages of this book, I want you to remember that you are beautiful and one-of-a-kind. You were made for a special purpose. You reflect the unrivaled work of your Master Craftsman. God certainly didn't make no *junk*! He sees you as a masterpiece and when you look in the mirror, He wants you to know that full-well. No matter what has occurred in your past, what is taking place currently, or in your future (read Jeremiah 29:11 again).

Be Healed, Be Equipped, and Be Restored!

~ *Tschanna M. Taylor*, MBA ~

Visionary Author
***H.E.R. Extreme Makeover*™ Founder**

H.E.R. Extreme Makeover™ Poem

By Evangelist Annie R. Davis-Lee

H – is for healing,
Whether it be in our body or the hurt within our soul.
He will touch the point of need and will truly make you whole.

E – is for equipping us,
Though we feel we can't endure, with the right strategies and tools to make us more confident and secure.

R – is for restoring.
He can turn our mess into a masterpiece.
A transformation occurs the moment you let go, forgive, and release.

TABLE OF CONTENTS

Dedication vi

Acknowledgements vii

Foreword by Nanette Floyd Patterson.. xi

Foreword by Felecia S. Killings xiii

Prologue xv

Introduction xx

H.E.R. Extreme Makeover™ Poem xxiii

Tschanna M. Taylor, MBA 1
   Mastering My Pieces: A Mess Turned into a Masterpiece

Christina Saunders 41
   Once a Fatherless Child

Erin Fuller-Russell 49
   Beautifully Broken

Tina L. Moore 55
   From Bitter to Blessed

Kier Ayers 63
   I Mastered the Art of Hiding

Shanae Starnes 71
   The Journey of My Voice's Revival

Angela Chance 79
   From Depression to Deliverance

Nakisha D. Blackwell 87
   Once Broken; Now Healed!

Cheryl Menifee 95
   Why Not Me?

Alisa J. Green 105
   My Mess and Masterpiece Through Love, Loss, and Business

Sharice Rush 113
   Married in Ministry

Conclusion 119

About the Compiler 122

How to Use This Book 124

Reflection Questions 126

So, What's Next? 129

Tschanna Taylor, "Your Purpose Strategist" 131

Connect with Tschanna 132

Books by Tschanna Taylor 133

Tschanna Taylor

H.E.R. Extreme Makeover

Tschanna M. Taylor, MBA

"The greatest asset in my pain is the power that it has to bring healing to the life of another, of which I myself am included."
~ Craig D. Lounsbrough ~

MASTERING MY PIECES: A MESS TURNED INTO A MASTERPIECE

The story you are about to read was written for **YOU**. You are not alone in your struggles. My purpose in writing this book is to show you that I am just as much of a "mess" as you are. The enemy uses our past to cause confusion and disorder in our lives. He is the recordkeeper of our history. He likes to torment us with feelings of guilt, doubt, fear, and condemnation. He is always trying to remind us of things that we have done to keep us from experiencing true healing.

That same enemy reminded me of awful occurrences in my life. He shamed and mocked me so much that guilt kept me chained. I felt that I was an exception to grace and couldn't be forgiven. However, I was reminded one Sunday after church that there are countless instances in the Bible where there are stories of all kinds of "hot messes" — people who were liars, thieves, adulterers, and others who were just full of "mess." If God could forgive them and use them for His purpose, surely, He could do the same for me!

Friend, the time has come for you to embrace the vision and purpose God has had for you all along, although you may have been unable to see through the "mess" of your past.

As you read this book, take some time to reflect on what resonates with you, makes you laugh, makes you cry, and/or has surprised you. I pray as you read the stories my co-authors and I share that your heart will be moved in an amazing way. We all are willing vessels, allowing God to turn our messes into masterpieces.

At the end of the book, you will find discussion questions so that you can journal your thoughts, grab a friend, or have a Saturday morning meeting with your intimate circle of friends. Discuss it. Have open conversations about it. Struggle through it. Why? Because I want you to take away the fact that it is okay not to be okay. In fact, it is my hope that you will begin to see how much you are loved amid your "mess."

Your "mess" can't and won't separate you from the Master Designer.

*You are a **MASTERPIECE!***

~~~~

DIVINELY DESIGNED

Think back for a moment to your childhood. When you were seven or eight years old, were you among the millions of little children who dreamed of being on top of the world? Did you ever dress up in your frilly dress and your mom's shoes? If someone told you that you were beautiful and fit for a handsome, nice guy, you wouldn't have argued. If someone were to say to you now that you are beautiful, you would shrink back.

Somewhere between childhood and adulthood, we lost that childlike confidence. As adults, we notice our flaws and compare ourselves with others, all while forgetting the beauty we possess in God's eyes.

To be human is to be "messy." It just goes with the territory. And let's be real: Some "messes" wash away. Some don't. This doesn't mean that you continue to be a victim or prisoner of the "mess." Break free and look for the message inside of the "mess." Share it with others!

We usually don't get excited about going through hard times. When trouble comes, it is easy to have an attitude that prompts one of the two following reactions:

1. *"Why is this happening to me?"* **OR**
2. *"This shouldn't be happening to me!"*

However, when we truly understand the value of our "messes," we can learn to go through them with joy. We often want to run or find ways to minimize our problems. Many times, we have no control over what happens to us or what happens in our lives. How we respond is where our power lies. We can either drown in despair or rise with the tide. Sometimes, things happen to provoke a change in us.

Our purpose—yours and mine—is to grow from our mistakes, to triumph over tragedy, and to allow God to make something beautiful out of our brokenness. There's absolutely nothing we can do that is so horrendous that He can't heal, equip, and restore. **NOTHING!**

We all have a story. We were all born with an incredible and innate gift to survive. Decide right now: Do you want to live a life by default or live life by design? Just as you were all those years ago, you are still beautiful today. That's what makes you *divinely designed!*

~~~~~

BACK IN THE DAY WHEN I WAS YOUNG—WHEN THE "MESS" STARTED EARLY

In order to move forward, over time, I have learned why it is so important to return to the beginning. True healing begins *HERE!* Through lots of therapy, coaching, and mentoring, I realized I was wearing a fancy mask. We all wear them…to a degree.

As a child, I was "conditioned" in a lot of areas in my life that carried over into my adulthood. My life was comprised of things such as *"Fake it 'til I make it," "Be a good little girl," "Go to school and get a good education," "Marry a man with money," "Stay quiet, chile so that you can keep this here man."* I was never taught financial literacy and being okay with playing second caused me to accept the status quo. What I learned, instead, was how to camouflage deep shame and pretend as if everything was okay in my life. For whatever the reason, many learn these same types of lessons in their childhood.

To be "authentic" means that you have to take some risks. Some people may not accept you—and that's okay. The beauty in being true to yourself will increase your self-esteem, personal dignity, and being unapologetic about your boldness and confidence.

For far too long, women have marched to the beat of someone else's drums. Reality shows seen on TV didn't just happen overnight; they actually go back as far as biblical times. Familiar names such as Eve, Rachel, Sarah, Esther, and Ruth are likely well-known to you. There are also women mentioned who you don't hear a lot about yet served as the "unsung heroine." They cooked their foods over open fires, carried their garbage to a dump, and drew their water from the river. Life and death occurred for them with no illicit drug use. Their life's lessons came from raw and unchartered places in their lives. Every situation they faced was indeed a "mess," but thanks be to God for Him creating their stories into a masterpiece. You, my friend, are no different.

As I go back to my beginning, I can't help but reminisce about a beautiful 15-year-old girl. Her skin was flawless with dimples wedged deeply in her face. She looked like a baby doll and was so childlike at heart. One day, she made a decision that would forever change her life: She got pregnant! (Back then, teenage pregnancy left girls feeling utter shame and embarrassment. Some kept their babies; others did not.) This young girl pushed through, regardless of the negative connotations she received from her mother and grandmother. Their harsh words affected her in such a way that her unborn baby received negative, degrading words before entry into this world. She would say things to the baby like, *"This is your fault!" "My life is over because of you!"* and *"You are nothing but a b***h, a whore, and a monster! I don't even want you."* For her child, rejection was already instilled from the very beginning based on the words spoken to her womb. (The baby's father eventually went about his business without a care in the world for mother or child.)

So, the 15-year-old soon met a man who was at least four years her senior. This man had his own set of issues when they met—so much so that he forced the 15-year-old's mother to sign a marriage certificate, threatening her life if she didn't approve.

The abuse then began. The 15-year-old gave birth but had no clue about how the story of her life would unfold.

That 15-year-old child I described was my mother when she was pregnant with me.

My mother was a beautiful woman by day, but by night, she was black and blue from the mental, verbal, and physical abuse from the man known as her husband. Sure, he was a provider for the family — but he made her work two jobs to provide for me. He was adamant that he wasn't going to do a lot for me because I wasn't "his child."

As I think back over the environment I grew up in, there was always a gloomy, dark spirit in our home. I can't remember a lot of fun times because we hardly went anywhere or took family vacations. There's only one time I can clearly recall going somewhere as a "family," and that was when we went to Charlotte, North Carolina to attend the Heritage USA theme park built by Televangelist Jim Bakker.

My friend's parents down the street from us would often ask our parents if we could come over to play. While visiting, we would play in our friend's treehouse, play tennis with our hands (we had no racquets), or go to the local high school football games.

I am forever grateful to James and Cheryl Carroll because I felt that they could "hear me" without me saying a single word of needing a reprieve.

There were many more painful moments than peaceful ones. This life recklessly planted seeds of hopelessness, fear, doubt, rejection, despair, hate, guilt, overwhelm, and frustration. I always felt I was placed in a caregiver role early on, left to feel guilty because I couldn't protect my mother.

I remember one time, in particular; it was her birthday. She was cooking dinner. When I heard him "invite" her to come to the bedroom, I knew it wasn't going to be good. His tone was very demanding and sharp. I ran to the hallway where the phone was mounted on the wall. I wasn't tall enough to reach the phone, so I grabbed a chair to climb on to turn the dial to 9-1-1. He must have heard me make a lot of noise because he ran out to see what I was doing. He then threatened me and said that if I called the police, he was going to hurt both my mom and me. *I was just a child!* **Who was going to protect me?** I felt like I was in prison. My mother eventually decided that enough was enough and left him after 16 years of marriage.

As a teenager, I was so terrified, lost, and unsure of who I was. High school was where I lost my sense of identity. In the 90s, you had to keep up with the latest fads such as wearing stirrups and an oversized shirt, overalls with your hat turned to the back, or the extra-large triangular earrings and chokers. This should have been a time of preparation for college and planning for my future after graduation. Instead, my mind was everywhere but in the books. I skipped school, was very sexually active, and hung out at the local parks when I should have been in school. With everything happening at home, this seemed to be my only way of escape.

I spiraled out of control. I didn't know how to voice my feelings because I couldn't trust anyone…not even my own mother. I had a lot of resentment and anger. I didn't understand why she made some of the decisions that she made. I had to mature at an early age and felt as if my childhood and teenage lives were stripped from me. My biological father was hardly around because he was spending his time singing background for a well-known gospel artist.

Now that I am older, more mature, and have a child of my own, I realize that at times, my mother did the best she could. I had to heal from those unresolved issues that had developed with her.

So, who could I turn to?

Two people in my life helped me cope with all of my crazy "mess": Mrs. Smith, the Guidance Counselor at my high school, and my great aunt, affectionately known as "Grandma." They both saw the significant changes within me (for the worse) and spent countless hours reaffirming me of my potential and that God was going to use me boldly as the voice to encourage others to excel in their purpose—but I couldn't "hear" them then. All I ever wanted was to be loved without shackles, but there were still issues I had to work through.

As a child, I had to comply with the demands and rules at home. This left me feeling rejected, uncertain about continuing to live life, confused, overwhelmed, sick (having been diagnosed with over 45 illnesses, symptoms, and conditions in my lifetime), exhausted, and voiceless. I've also encountered two failed marriages, two failed businesses, and a lot of debt—all from feeling I had to "prove myself."

As I listened to my friends share their experiences with their parents, I felt embarrassed about my family life and would lie just to "fit in." My mother and I were blamed as if everything wrong were our fault. This seed left me feeling as if I always had to prove myself to others. This thinking led to negative behaviors: careless sex, domestic violence in my own relationships (even though I vowed I would never tolerate it after seeing my mother go through), drinking alcohol, emotional eating, and frivolous spending.

Have you ever felt so tired of being sick and tired until finally, you stomp your foot and realize that enough is enough? I was there! I needed to let go and be free!

Childhood may seem so long ago, but the things experienced as a child can significantly affect your adulthood. When you experience a major rejection, it will show up later on in life. Sometimes, you will find yourself making negative assumptions about what others think about you. You end up being a people pleaser. You may get weary about letting people in to shield yourself from any more hurt and have a difficult time trusting others with your feelings.

However, there is hope! You can overcome any type of insecurity that stems from childhood. You must first recognize the problem and go back to the beginning to live in the solution. Decide not to take so many things personally. Recognize that you can't change what happened "back then," but you can change how you react to the situation. Remove any patterns that were started in the beginning, take consistent action, and learn from the experience.

Those past events became my identity. If, after all, that is all you see every day, you unknowingly become a by-product of your environment. That conditioning caused me to stay stuck and was definitely a huge "mess." My childhood afflictions prepared me for much more intense challenges to come.

All My Life, I Had to Fight!

In the movie *The Color Purple*, there is an infamous part that Orpah Winfrey (Ms. Sophia) shared with Whoopi Goldberg (Celie Harris) when she said, *"All my life, I had to fight!"* This part in the movie resonates with my life. Fighting was of no appeal to me, but it was necessary if I were to be victorious. I've had to fight my identity issues, confidence levels, family issues, fear, doubt, health challenges, my own mind, and while in relationships, too.

My identity had been swallowed up in putting others before myself. There were internal voices that asked questions such as, *"What will people think?" "Will they be upset if I don't do this?"* I harbored a lot of anxieties because I lacked the encouragement or motivation to do anything positive, had no example of real love (leaving me with a sense of unknowing what to expect), and drama all the time.

Did you have to fight a lot while growing up?

~~~~~

God Always Provides You with a Way of Escape

I got married immediately after high school and relocated to Jersey City, New Jersey. At the time, I thought I was going to leave all of my problems with the family behind. Little did I know that I literally jumped from one frying pan into another! I learned that going to another state wasn't going to solve my problems at home.

Sidebar: *Deal with the problems at home because they will follow you—no matter what state you are in.*

After being married for only six months, I was in a dangerous "mess" once again. This time, I found myself being pinned down on the couch while the pressure of his knees felt like they were connected to my ribs. The doctors told me I would never have children due to the abuse.

I received a call that my great-grandmother passed away. This was my way of escape. I returned home to attend the funeral, leaving all of my personal belongings behind. My peace was more important than that "stuff." At times, I felt guilty by staying longer than I said I would and eventually decided to stay in Durham. I got a job and moved into my own place.

A year after my great-grandmother's passing, I moved on with my life and met a guy through a high school friend. We hit it off well. After dating for a year and a half, we moved in together. Who knew there were a lot of lessons I needed to learn in this next "mess"?

~~~~~

Why Buy the Cow When the Milk is Free?

My grandmother was a former pastor, and my grandfather was a bishop. I got saved at 14 years old. When they started their church, I was the church's secretary. Grandma always had a way to slide in scriptures, quotes, sayings, and clichés into her conversations. Sometimes, they would get on my nerves! Now, I appreciate all the times she shared with me things that I wish I would have listened to and took what she said seriously.

The one saying she said that stands out the most was, *"Why would he buy the cow when he is getting the milk for free?"* I was so lost. I was trying to figure out why she was talking in riddles…**and where was this cow?** Frustrated, I avoided her at all costs because I didn't want to hear any more about how I was wrong for "shacking up." I can't even lie. *It felt umm umm good!* While living together, my boyfriend lost his job and decided to start a career in the trucking industry. He would be away from the home for three to four months at a time and, when he would return home, would stay for only a few days to no more than two weeks.

All the clues were there; I just chose not to see them. Women would call the house and hang up when I answered. Underwear that didn't belong to me would appear in his gym bag or in the truck—something I would notice when he invited me to ride with him across the United States.

I refused to believe he had checked out on me. I was so naïve at the time and started reasoning with myself: *I would rather have a piece of man than to have all of him!* Now, how silly was that? Have you ever been there, done that before?

Then came the lies and excuses. He would call home to say he would be home in a few days and the day that he was scheduled to return, he would say he picked up extra loads to make more money. I was in college full-time and decided not to work to focus on school, so my educational venture occupied a majority of my time. It was at this moment when I realized I was giving him wifely benefits when he didn't rank up to husband status. Bills were getting further and further behind. He had stopped sending money home to cover the bills.

I didn't want to go back home to live with my mother to hear her negative comments, so I started looking for a job and put my education on hold. I got a temp job working for a local hospital. My job was to be a Sterile Processing Tech, responsible for decontaminating, inspecting, assembling, packaging, and sterilizing medical instruments used in the operating room. I loved the job and my co-workers, but I didn't enjoy looking at a lot of blood, veins, and bone fragments. Lord knows I pushed through because I had to pay those bills!

At the same time, my biological father got terminally ill and spent his last days in the hospital where I worked. When I was little, my stepfather made sure I didn't spend a lot of time with my father. Sometimes, my father would come to my school so that we could catch up and spend time together. When I was old enough, I vowed that nothing or no one was going to keep me away from my father. It's funny how my mother and some family members always had something negative to say about my biological father but didn't stand up for us when it came to dealing with the issues my stepfather presented. So, I was afforded the opportunity to spend as much time as possible with my father because our time was very limited.

A month passed, and I hadn't heard a thing from my boyfriend. It was fine, though. I was focused on my father and my job. When the disconnect notices started coming in, I took matters into my own hands and got really stupid. I was careless, and eventually, my foolish ways caught up with me.

My life quickly spiraled out of control. My father passed away. I finally heard from my boyfriend, but he seemed "distant." I was angry because he wasn't there for me at my father's funeral. Our conversation was limited because I didn't have much to say to him. I had shut down. Somehow, he managed to feed me a bunch of sweet nothings, and I gave him another chance. It must be noted here that we still hadn't discussed how we were going to tackle the bills.

One Thursday, when I arrived at work, I wasn't even there for an hour before I was called to the office. I was informed that two detectives were waiting for me on the unsterile side of the processing unit where I worked. I was told that my timesheets didn't add up and that I was caught obtaining property under false pretenses. I was fired from the job and told by the detectives that since it was my first offense, I was instructed to meet them on my own recognizance at the Sheriff's department downtown.

My heart raced like it was about to jump clean out of my chest. All sorts of thoughts raced through my head. The biggest one was knowing that I might as well get ready for my own funeral because my mother was going to kill me, even though I was an adult. The other concern I had was that I had four cousins who worked for the Sheriff's department. I knew that if my mother didn't find out immediately, they would see me there and call her. Either way, I was "dead."

When I arrived at the Sheriff's department, I went through the process of being fingerprinted and booked. The crime I committed was a Class H felony! I managed to breathe a huge sigh of relief to learn that all of my cousins were off that day. That factor still didn't mean that much because they could have seen my name when they came in the next day. I called my grandma to help me with this situation. She prayed and, after her prayer, I felt like everything was going to be okay. I knew what I had done could have me locked up for a minimum of 25 months. *I didn't serve any jail time.* I was, however, arrested. I had to go to court, plead guilty to the crime I committed, perform 200 hours of community service, and have at least 12 months of regular contact with my probation officer. I completed my community service working at the Veterans Affairs Hospital and the YMCA. I also paid back the restitution I had incurred.

As a felon, it was difficult finding a job. No one would hire me. While going through all of this, I recall saying, *"I will never work for another fast-food restaurant ever again!"* The day I completed my service with probation and looked for work (only to be rejected at every turn), I was left with no other choice but to take a job working in fast-food at the Chick-Fil-A in the mall.

Sidebar: *Be careful of the words you speak. You may not realize just how powerful they are.*

Ex-female offenders frequently face rejection, being told no, encounter repeated setbacks, and are consistently ignored. Frustrated, I decided to start a nonprofit organization focused on serving African-American ex-female offenders with experience in the prison system who were trying to rebuild their lives, share H.E.R. stories, and teach them basic entrepreneurial skills. Although my incident with the correctional system was unique and nowhere near as harsh as others, it doesn't change the fact that I knew and encountered the same types of struggles. I will **NEVER FORGET!**

When Two Becomes One

You would think that after the first fiasco, I would have learned my lesson. I didn't. I had created patterns that were obviously a problem, but I couldn't see it. I didn't know I needed to heal from the patterns I saw while growing up as a child regarding relationships. In marriage, nothing is more important than growing into real maturity and getting rid of childlike patterns. Too many people enter into marriage thinking, communicating, and understanding like children.

How did I know if I really loved him or not? Was I really trying to find something that was missing from my previous relationship?

Well, after four years, being married to a person who no longer "rang my bell" almost cost me my life. The greatest problem in this marriage was the lack of communication. I experienced manipulative mind games, intimidation, and mental, emotional, and verbal abuse which equated to being knocked around, kicked, and stomped on. Think about it. If he came in with his own set of issues and I came in with mine, the two shall become one. He and I had some straight-up issues!

How do children communicate? Some do so with cruel, harsh, sharp, and hurtful words. Some don't say anything at all. Remember the saying, *"Sticks and stones may break my bones, but words will never hurt me"*? Whoever came up with that saying **LIED!** In reality, words **DO** hurt—and the pain can be intense.

My ex-husband was cruel and harsh, where I felt like I couldn't open my mouth to voice my feelings. The first thing to recognize is that the fruit in our lives comes from somewhere.

Bad fruit comes from trees with bad roots. Being married to a Deacon meant that I had a lot of "fake it 'til I make it" moments, especially when we were in church. It shocked me how people would walk up to me after church and tell me to my face that I looked so unhappy, yet I lied to save face for him. I was miserable. I hated going home. I would sometimes sit in the driveway for at least an hour before walking in the house. I couldn't be intimate anymore because I was so beat down verbally, mentally, and emotionally. I tried to talk to him about seeking marital counseling, but he was adamant that he wasn't going to speak to anyone about anything.

One day, I was at work, and as I exited the bathroom stall to wash my hands, a lady approached me. I did not know this woman and had never seen her in the building before. Next thing I knew, she started prophesying to me. At first, it seemed like the same "word" I would always hear about God blessing me. I knew she was real when she became very specific about me praying and asking the Lord to remove me from my situation. She shared with me that the Lord heard me and that He made a way of escape…but I went back. She went on to say that He would allow me to go again but that this time, I must stay gone or else I would end up dead. (That part I knew to be true because the week before this prophecy, the Deacon got upset after I told him I was leaving—and he pulled a rifle on me. I was scared to death because I had never had a gun pulled on me before.) So, as I tuned in to what she was sharing directly from the Lord, she gave me the exact plan of how to move away from my situation.

It didn't take anyone having to tell me for the third time what to do. I was out of there and left nothing of mine behind.

Eventually, he started stalking me and located where I had relocated to in another town an hour away from where he and I lived while together. I ended up getting a restraining order, thinking it would protect me. It didn't. He was eventually arrested for violating the restraining order—and I was left to file for bankruptcy. We divorced and moved on with our lives.

As humans, we are designed to engage in meaningful relationships. Despite the difficulties we have with relationships—whether intimate, professional, or familial—they are still a gift because we are relational beings. When we choose to work through the rough spots and commit to loving others, we reap the benefits.

When we invest our time and emotions into a relationship, allowing ourselves to be vulnerable and trusting, there are bound to be times when we will get hurt. We are imperfect. None of us are immune from being hurt or hurting others. The truth of the matter is that no matter how strong our friendship bonds are, without forgiveness and communication, every one of our relationships would be short-lived! However, forgiveness can be tricky. It can be difficult to determine if you've truly forgiven someone. Can you relate? Although extending forgiveness to another may or may not make a difference to that person, that is not the primary reason we do it. Through forgiveness, we mend our own brokenness and, in letting go, we deepen our relationship with God by turning over the hurt.

So, there I was **AGAIN**...in a "mess"! The answer was to move forward. God had already prepared me for the life I was living. It was time to stop making decisions based upon what I was lacking and to make some based on all I had access to. God doesn't put more on us than we can bear. He makes the path clear for us; we just have to stop allowing someone else's issues to affect the outcome of our own lives.

~~~~~

Heal Me So That I Can R.E.L.A.X.

OUCH, LIFE! Why are you so rough on me? Remember earlier in the book when I shared that you have to go back to the beginning? Well, this is true for every area of our lives, even our health. Every issue we face started somewhere. These reoccurring problems come to steal, kill, and destroy us from being free and happy. We must identify the problem, consent to receive healing, and make the necessary changes, all while trusting your process. Why? Because healing is a **PROCESS!** There are no quick fixes. If you allow him to, the enemy loves to keep you trapped in a prison of guilt and shame. He knows how to make us feel worthless and responsible (in a bad way) for the choices we make.

Have you ever noticed that some of the issues you deal with (i.e., anger, sickness, frustration, overwhelm, poverty, divorce, depression, debt, failed relationships, dishonor, stress, and anxiety—to name a few) are conditions that started generations before you? They are learned behaviors (see Exodus 20:5).

We have grown to be who we are at this very moment because of what we've been through, where we've been, and the people we've met. When you grow up poor, barely having your needs met, or when you grow up without your father or mother, it can be tough to stand on your own. You learned to depend on yourself more than you can rely on others. You became hardworking, which can sometimes lead to being a perfectionist. Risks and opportunities had to be taken to reach your dreams of creating a comfortable life.

For years, a tug-of-war took place in my heart and mind. One day, I nearly gave in to the tactics of the enemy because I was at a breaking point. I believed that I was insignificant and worthless. I got tired of being sick and tired. I wanted a change in my life!

At some point in our lives, we have all experienced being lied on, lied to, cut corners, shifted blame, hurt from others, hurt others, held grudges…and I could easily continue naming things. However, it is a blessing to know that no matter our "mess," God can *redefine, affirm,* and *rebuild* them into a masterpiece. You are a survivor and a fighter, resilient in your conviction of life. This is what kept your hope alive, along with the few who showed you love. Whatever the "mess," it is not your fault. Learn to **R.E.L.A.X.!**

R*ecognize* the burdens that weigh you down

and affect your health.

E*liminate* toxic thoughts and relationships.

L*et* it go (forgive quickly).

Change your **A***ttitude.*

Get some **X***tra* sleep.

Release those burdens that hinder you emotionally, physically, energetically, financially, and spiritually!

~~~~~

Finger Pricks and Over This Mess!

As early as the age of 17, I knew something was wrong with me but couldn't quite put my finger on it. I told my mother about the different symptoms, and she dismissed them all as if they were just issues going on in my head. I also called my grandmother for advice on what to do, and she would simply tell me to take a nap. No one took me seriously—and I was *frustrated!*

In 2000, after experiencing severe pains from an ectopic pregnancy, I was diagnosed with gestational diabetes that developed into full-blown diabetes. It took me at least ten years to accept that diagnosis, even though most of my family had the condition. I didn't follow any of the diets or plans given to me. I would buy medicine…and not take it (now, that was a "mess" by itself). I even went as far as lying on my logbook to make it look like I had the perfect numbers, too silly to realize that the quarterly A1c tests showed my truths. I was not honest with **MYSELF** about it all. I ate what I wanted to eat and cringed when people would 'check me' to tell me *"I shouldn't eat this"* or *"I shouldn't eat that."* I was on a self-destructive path. Family members have died from this disease. I've had friends in their 20s die from this disease. I've seen the people in the community who walked around town with their white canes dipped in red paint at the tips as they tapped their way around. I've seen others who've had to use wheelchairs because of an amputated leg or foot attributed to this disease. You would *think* that with all of that exposure, it would be a wake-up call to me. It wasn't.

It was only a matter of time before my diabetes would get so out of control that it caused me to have emergency laser eye surgery to save my retina from detaching. There were a lot of sleepless nights from nausea and vomiting, leg cramps, blurred vision, and not being motivated to do anything about the damage I brought onto myself.

In my lifetime, I have suffered from or been diagnosed with:

- Asthma
- Six Miscarriages
- Ulcers
- Bronchitis
- Acid Reflux
- Cervical Cancer
- Migraines
- Polycystic Ovary Syndrome
- High Cholesterol
- High Blood Pressure
- Low/High Blood Sugars
- Urinary Infections
- Diabetic Retinopathy
- Diabetes
- Diabetic Neuropathy
- Sexual Dysfunction
- Restless Leg Syndrome
- Gastroparesis
- Nonfatty Liver Disease
- Depression

- ❖ Stomach Pains
- ❖ Hiatal Hernia
- ❖ Anemia
- ❖ Mood Swings
- ❖ Anxiety
- ❖ Constipation
- ❖ Fibroids
- ❖ Infertility
- ❖ Carpal Tunnel Syndrome
- ❖ Nervous Breakdown

I have **NO** doubt you are saying, *"GOOD LORD!"* Yes, my friend: These issues really happened to me — **ALL** of them. I am no longer being affected by the vast majority of them; although there are some I still deal with daily.

Your past can spill over into your present. It can affect you physically, along with the way you think. People often times express that they want to change, but they are not actually ready. As a result of doing nothing, nothing changes! Then, they complain. *"Nothing's changed!"* Really, though? Well, guess what? That used to be me. My beliefs were all jacked up!

Think about this: We are the ones who create most of the roadblocks in our lives. Our own preconceptions and limiting beliefs can hinder us from reaching the success, healing, and fulfillment for which we are seeking. Acknowledging this and moving to learn more about yourself can help with unblocking the flow of life that you are authentically meant to live.

As for me, I was too cool to admit that I had a problem deeper than my physical ailments. In actuality, I was scared, confused, and overwhelmed. Most people can recall their moments in time when they were ill. Me? I can't remember a time when I felt good back then.

Life is undoubtedly about choices. Like it or not, you are 100% responsible for your life. If you haven't lost weight, it's on **YOU**. If you haven't done everything expected of you to maintain your healing, yep: That's on **YOU!** We all come into this world the same way, but the life we end up with is based on the *choices* we make.

Growing up in Durham meant going to McDonald's on Saturdays at the age of seven. I then graduated from a Kid's Meal to a #1 Combo: Big Mac, fries, soda, and an apple pie to top things off. Sundays after church, we would immediately go to the local buffets or wait for grandma to finish rolling the dough to drop into the pot of boiled chicken to make chicken and dumplings. In the African-American community, traditional foods have cultural, social, and spiritual significance. Many of the members do what they need to do to put food on the table, pushing all health concerns to the back burner.

The Bible tells us that we (as a people) suffer for the lack of knowledge—but even when we know, we reject it. We won't apply it. What they would joke about by calling diabetes "The Sugar" or a person being "A Diabetical" loses its humor when you see someone's name in the obituary section of the newspaper, or you hear *"Brother or Sister So-and-So is in the hospital because they had a foot or leg amputated."* My mother died at the age of 49 after having five strokes and five heart attacks. My father died at the age of 42 from a brain tumor and complications from diabetes. I could continue to name the countless number of family, church members, and friends who have died from this disease or complications from it.

I tried every fad diet there is. Slim Fast. Hydroxycut. B12 injections. Medi Weight Loss. WeightNot Therapeutic Nutrition Coaching. Fasting. Intermittent fasting. And more. One Sunday, I went to the altar at church for prayer concerning my health. After prayer, the minister said, *"If you continue to do and eat as you want, why are you continuing to come up for prayer?"* It was tight but right. That day, I knew God was sending a warning before destruction.

~~~~

ICU Was the Final Straw for Me to Get My Entire Life in Order

I could no longer blame how I was raised on my health because I had become an adult. It goes back to being 100% responsible for your own life. Everything in our life happens for a reason. Purpose is in the "mess."

Four months after my prayer request in church, I started having excruciating stomach pains and feeling as if I was locked up. I made an appointment with a Gastroenterologist where I had to eat radioactive eggs and drink a radioactive liquid. This procedure was performed to determine that I had gastroparesis—a condition that affects how the muscles in the stomach propel food through the digestive tract. I developed gastroparesis from poor diabetes management and other medicines working against each other within my body. Can you imagine sitting to try and get relief by grabbing your ankles or singing songs like, *"I Was Locked Up; They Won't Let Me Out"* or *"Break Every Chain"*? What about quotes from movies like *Amistad*: *"Let There Be Free"*? I'm really not being comical here, even though you are probably falling out of your chair, but this is the best description that I can give to how I was feeling.

NOTHING WORKED *(Tschanna slaps her forehead in frustration).* I tried detox teas, laxatives, smooth moves, magnesium citrate, water, enemas…**NOTHING WHATSOEVER WORKED!** I thought I was going to lose my mind! LOL!

Then came the uncontrollable vomiting that would "just happen" out of nowhere. It was so bad, my son would rush to bring me a plastic grocery store bag and say, *"Here, mommy. Here is your emergency kit."* I was so embarrassed about him seeing me that way. I remember being on the highway headed to work and almost causing an accident behind trying to quickly find something to capture my vomiting episode. Thankfully, I made my way across the lanes safely and pulled over to the shoulder. I cried out of sheer frustration and apologized to myself for not taking better care of myself than I had.

I scheduled another appointment with the Gastroenterologist and was told that if I didn't do an emergency Gastric Bypass surgery, I would die from dehydration. After discussing this dire situation with my family, we all agreed that I should move forward with the operation.

I'm grateful that the surgery went well. Two days after, the doctors did their hospital rounds. On this particular morning, there were more doctors on staff than usual. My room was crowded as they stood and hovered over me, asking if I was okay and whispering among themselves. I was nervous because I didn't know what was going on. They told me that they needed to rush me to the Intensive Care Unit (ICU) because my left lung had collapsed and they couldn't figure out why everything seemed to be so normal for me. The news scared me so bad, I instantly went into shock and blacked out.

At that moment, I heard a voice I hadn't distinctly heard in a long time: God's. He told me it was His way of finally slowing me down from taking care of everyone else's needs while neglecting my own. He said He was going to streamline my life. That meant He would have to remove people and things that didn't serve my purpose any longer. The instructions He gave me were very clear and specific. He explained that all of the lessons I learned in life were for a reason and that He wanted to heal me as far back as my childhood. I was instructed to write down every person who treated me bad, lied on me, stole from me, and a laundry list of other things I didn't even realize I was holding on to that caused me bitterness and pain. Those experiences are what God will use for my future, to share my testimony of life's *"Messes"* turned into *"Masterpieces"* so that others can be free and share their stories. This is where the **H.E.R. Extreme Makeover™ Movement** was formed.

God has entrusted us to honor, care for, nurture, and grow what He has given to each of us. He has equipped us with the tools to develop by letting go of any hurts from the past and releasing any inherited or generational thoughts, values, and beliefs. We are to accept 100% responsibility for the choices we make.

Remember this moment of choosing to commit to knowing and growing yourself to a path of healing. Promise yourself that once you start, there is no turning back. Do not allow excuses to keep you chained from living life at 100%. Condition your mind to be ready for any and everything. There are infinite possibilities in your healing process.

Oh! And *trust* your process. The people or situations that occurred are not mere coincidences, either. Where you have been, what you have been through, the choices you have made, and the people who impacted your life were all necessary for you to build your character. Those life skills and exercises helped you "mature" into the person you are today. Stress is an essential component as well. Although stress can be helpful to move us on our growth path, it can also be hurtful when you are exposed to it for a long time. Be honest and confident with yourself. Recognize the blockages you have placed on yourself that shackle your growth. Learn the reason behind those blockages and work vehemently to unbind, unlock, and unleash them.

Pain is a part of life. Many times, what we perceive as difficult or painful may just be what we need to better ourselves. When chronic pain or illness shows up, it can be a sign to upgrade your life.

Sidebar: *We are all here to help one another.*

We all have something in our lives that has damaged our hearts or self-esteem, but God can always transform something ugly into something beautiful. He can turn ashes into beauty and brokenness into purpose. All things are possible…if you believe. Do you believe that? Change your position to change your condition!

~~~~~

MINDSET MAKEOVER

It took me years and a lot of hard-won experiences from the struggles of being imprisoned in my mind. Opportunities flew past me because of feeling like I wasn't good enough, important enough, or that others' opinions of me mattered.

When I look back at all of my early mistakes, stuck moments, and missed opportunities due to fear and doubt, they really helped propel me to **WAKE UP!** I was in a dire situation. I had no idea what to do, where to go, or how to get there. I only knew that doing things the same way wasn't getting me different results. Instead, I was more burnt out and frustrated. I knew there had to be *something* else that my success heroes understood that I had yet to grasp for myself.

When I started asking the right questions, I started getting the right answers (coaching my own self). There are two types of mindsets:

1. The ones who accept their situations and remain stuck.
2. Those who go "all in" while being scared to death, yet willing to risk it all.

The latter can manifest in so many ways. I was trapped "investing" in myself, holding on to limited beliefs that I could only reach a certain place just to be more focused than when I first started. Today, I can say that I have a free mindset and follow God's path for my life via other successful people who are my mentors. I now reject the mindset that I can only achieve based on what I know. Instead, I can seek to learn, evolve, and grow all the time!

I know a lot of individuals who shrink away or stay stuck due to a lack of focus, drive, determination, perseverance, anxiety, stress, debt, and other financial woes instead of reaching and creating the life they truly want. I learned these principles from life's lessons and have experienced both mindsets at one point or another.

At the age of 18, I started my first business: Event planning. Back then, there was no such thing as "coaches." All I had was the people in the community who rooted me on. I had no one to hold me accountable for the goals I had set. I didn't know what to do or how to do it. I just knew I wanted to be a **B-O-S-S**, especially after working several dead-end jobs. I was adamant that there had to be a better life than what I was living at the time. I would naively give my products away for free, thinking that people would pay later (like the "Wimpy Method" on the old *Popeye* cartoon *("I'd gladly pay you Tuesday for a hamburger today))*.

Sidebar: *No matter how long you've been in business, you will always encounter someone who thinks you should give away your skills for free.*

I had to learn how to handle requests for "free service," but it first started with me and areas in my life that needed healing. I had to break down internal blocks and limiting beliefs. These were energy-drainers, too. I had to get quiet and meditate on figuring out what I was afraid of and what was holding me back. I had to be open to what I learned and apply it in my life if I wasn't ready yet to throw in the towel for my business.

When life's circumstances are not always joyous or positive, we can decide how we think about them. No one can succeed if they don't think they can. That was how I thought. I was fearful and afraid that I wouldn't make it and yes, I had **two** failed businesses — but I didn't allow that to keep me from trying again.

Your mindset — whether positive or negative — is determined by your response to external forces and attitudes. Regardless of how your day is going, it doesn't take much to throw us into a negative mind spin. No internet connection. A snide remark. Traffic jams. It doesn't take much to get us off track. You do, however, have the power within to make a change.

Life is a strategy. You have to find out who you are, what you are called to do, and how you will implement what you've learned to share it with others.

It all starts, plays out, and finishes in the mind. Below, I share strategies for you to consider when renewing your mind (read Romans 12:2):

- ❖ Address your fears.
- ❖ Have some fun.
- ❖ Seek opportunities all around you.
- ❖ Set strong boundaries and don't cave in.
- ❖ Discover what your purpose is and take action to move forward.
- ❖ Be okay with taking risks. There's always a blessing in the lesson — and you will have plenty of lessons!

- ❖ Connect with others (aka your tribe, circle, sisterhood/brotherhood, village, or community).
- ❖ Accept 100% responsibility for how you respond. Do not shift the blame.
- ❖ Communicate effectively.
- ❖ Show gratitude daily.
- ❖ Think of the situation as a challenge, not a problem (change how you view it).
- ❖ Learn from your mistakes.
- ❖ Overcome procrastination, fear, and doubt.
- ❖ Create a plan. Assess and rework your plan as needed.
- ❖ RELAX!

In the midst of your storms, it's important to take inventory of your thoughts and release any that are stealing your peace. We are each created differently, perfectly adapted for the specific call on our lives. Renew your mind. Renew your thinking. Renew your life!

~~~~~

THE ROYAL MASTERPIECE MAKEOVER— WHAT'S IN YOUR MAKEUP KIT?

To become the beautiful person you are meant to be, you must understand that your process takes preparation. In the book *Professional Woman: Self-Esteem, Confidence & Empowerment*, I share my story "Purpose Blueprint" that discusses how each of us is uniquely designed for a purpose. Before we can live a life of purpose, we must first discover it. Purpose is vigilant and will push you to stay up late, making sacrifices to meet goals that you have set. Purpose requires a commitment to the vision that is larger than ourselves, even when you are ready to throw in the towel. You must have a blueprint. A "blueprint" is a plan or model of something, usually in the form of a map.

> *"Many are the plans of a person's heart, but it is the Lord's plans that prevail."*
> **~ Proverbs 19:21 ~**

We were created to create. Similar to the architect who uses a blueprint to construct a house, we should utilize the same techniques to pursue the purpose of our lives.

I will further explain this same technique with how we use makeup daily. I am no makeup artist, but I have taken a few classes on applying makeup. In my 20s, I used to sell Mary Kay products. I never thought the techniques I used to enhance my beautifulness could be a teaching tool for those I serve.

There are no right or wrong ways to apply makeup. You have to do what's best for you (similar to your life). I want you to take the natural way of makeup application and apply it to you spiritually checking out what is in your makeup kit.

When God created you as His masterpiece, He created a beautiful, exquisite creation. First, before you apply any makeup, you must wash your face to cleanse it, but what God wants you to do is cleanse your heart from every hurt, every pain, every negative spoken word, and every negative thought (read Psalm 51:7-10 & 1 John 1:9).

Next, if you're like me, I prefer liquid foundation over powder foundation (be sure to use an SPF foundation for your skin type that includes sunscreen *(SONscreen)* protection). The foundation provides good coverage, similar to God serving as our foundation to rebuild us. This preparation for the shine of His glory is what will be used to reveal your story and mine to other women (read 2 Corinthians 3:18).

The blemishes on my face need a concealer, depending on the type of event I am planning to attend (this factor will determine whether or not I use a concealer). It is here when I seek God for forgiveness for myself and for those who have caused me pain. Why? Because God can conceal every hurt to turn my ashes into beauty. You don't have to hide anything. God got you! It's okay to let this stuff go!

Now, I don't know about what you use, but I have at least seven different brushes (I guess that's because it's what I learned when I took the makeup class). I have to have my blender brush, concealer brush, blush brush, brow brush, eyeshadow brush, powder brush, and lip brush. Lovingly, God shared with me the importance of staying grounded in Ephesians 6:10-19, putting on the whole armor of God.

Next, we will move on to the eyeshadows. The eyeshadows served as a reminder that no matter what my "mess" was, I could look to the hills for my help because all of my help comes from the Lord. When we place our focus on other things that don't really serve us, we could sometimes apply the wrong type of shade or use the improper technique. This is no different than life. Be careful of what you allow in because the eyes are the windows into your soul (read Proverbs 23:7).

Then, we select the cheek and lip color. With our lips, we should give God thanks and praise as well as speak encouraging words over ourselves and others (see Ephesians 4:29). I had to laugh because lately, I have been quite vociferous of an issue that occurred on my job.

Keep your makeup kit with you at all times because you never know when you have to do some retouches here or there. The same holds true for life.

Be very mindful of the tools in your toolkit. So many times, we focus on making sure the outer is beautiful, or we go by what we see on TV, looking to see if we are the right shape, weight, or have the latest designer signature bag or stylish shoe with the rhinestones on top—but we do little for our inner selves. This is the time to get quiet and think, meditate, pray, and administer self-care. There is no amount of makeup that can help you feel beautiful if you are emotionally, physically, and spiritually bankrupt. You are a work of art, a masterpiece, a valuable original, a one-of-a-kind (read Ephesians 2:10).

Here are some things I'd like for you to stop doing:

1. Stop being afraid of what others think. When you do this, you violate your integrity.
2. Stop lying to yourself, to God, and to others.
3. Stop putting others' needs before your own.
4. Stop denying overwhelm, frustration, confusion, and fear. You never have to pretend. Feel your feelings by thinking things through, but also take action!
5. Stop blaming. Although at times, it can be comfortable, it strips away the power from your life. Be 100%

responsible for your life. Set boundaries and be okay with saying no.
6. Stop overworking yourself. Get some rest.
7. Stop speaking negatively over yourself. Doing so is contagious and when others hear you do it, they sometimes "follow the leader."
8. Stop comparing yourself to others. We all have been **tagged**; given *talents*, *abilities*, *gifts*, more *gifts*, *experiences*, and *definitive* skills. Use them! Never second-guess yourself or overthink it. It's too stressful trying to keep up with the demands of others. Be free!

~~~~~

THE ULTIMATE MAKEOVER

So, now that you have read some of my "mess," what do you think? Do you seriously believe that your "mess" is worse? Now, I do know that my stories may not be as serious to some, but they are real and did happen to me.

Just as we would never toss our children away, God would never throw His children away, either. He desires to *heal* us, *equip* us, and *restore* us—just as He promised in 2 Corinthians 5:17. Look at the woman accused of adultery in John 8:1-5. The crowd had it in for her. They considered her a throwaway. She was a woman who made mistakes and should be held accountable for her actions, but Jesus saw a masterpiece. In biblical times, it was customary to accuse people publicly of adultery, but the law also said that the man and the woman had to be accused together. In this particular biblical account, the man was nowhere to be found. Jesus was so strategic, though. He stooped down to write in the dust—not once, but **TWICE**—and what he quietly wrote (as the accusers yelled and demanded answers) made them all "eat their dust." They had no room to question anything. I share this same sentiment with you. Stop shrinking back from the negative talks of others about you. Stop carrying other people's "mess" like you're some type of trash can. There are two lessons we can get from this story:

1. None of us are perfect; and
2. Despite our "messes," they can be turned into masterpieces.

Be willing to trust your process. The past is the past, but your purpose is built upon it and paves the way for a beautiful future. If God can use the sharing of my past experiences to help even one person escape a prison of shame and regret, surely, He can do the same for you!

What an undeserved privilege it has been to write and speak about my life and witness the power of healing, equipping, and restoring. It's likely that your situation is entirely different from mine. What a gift it is to watch women for the very first time as their prison walls crumble around them, never to be erected again.

Over the years, I have met a lot of women who were sexually abused as a child or violently raped by a stranger, secretly drowning in a sea of disgrace, embarrassment, and degradation—feeling like a throwaway. These issues cause a lot of pain psychologically, emotionally, and spiritually, which leads to worthlessness, shame, helplessness, depression, and even thoughts of suicide. Sadly, this happens every day. What I do know is that God can heal the most damaged heart. I have heard the stories of countless women who deal with weight issues, not being able to control what or how much they are eating, coupled with a lack of willpower while feeling critical and discouraged about themselves. I have spoken to some who resorted to using pills to take away their pain or drink alcohol, some who have served prison time, some who feel lonely although they are married, or those who feel incomplete due to a messy divorce. Some women had affairs or were victims of their spouse's infidelities, leaving them feeling unwanted. Then, there were some who gave their all in the church, leaving them burned out and their marriages or relationships suffered dearly for it.

In all of those circumstances, shame can get a good grip on you, which paralyzes you from moving forward to your healing and purpose. Unfortunately, these powerful emotions—regardless of the painful circumstances that caused them—result in not only doubting our own self-worth but also doubting whether we are worthy in God's sight. They build walls too high to see or get over, causing us to regress continually, which is really a sign of distrust in God.

If you have ever struggled with self-condemning thoughts or find it difficult to believe God can turn your "mess" into a masterpiece, let's take some time to dispel those thoughts so that you can move forward in your purpose. Each one of us can be used for a great purpose. In specific ways, He has equipped each of us to do amazing things through the painful experiences we have endured.

The pages that follow explore ten personal testimonies of life's "messes" turned into masterpieces, from daddy being absent, and married to ministry, to failed businesses and relationships. While each story builds upon the next and is meant to be read in the order presented, each story also stands alone. You may wish to begin with a story that speaks urgently to your present circumstance. Once you've read that story, I encourage you to return to the beginning and understand how the content fits into your life. Please know that you do not have to figure things out alone.

This will be the perfect opportunity for you to talk about and practically apply this material. Second, find and rely on wise, experienced mentors or coaches to guide you through the complexities of your "mess."

Queen, strategies are necessary for your *"Masterpiece Makeover"!*

Christina Saunders

"The pain that you have been feeling can't compare to the joy that is coming."
~ Romans 8:18 ~

Dedication
I dedicate this to my mother. Mommy, I love you! To all the mothers and daughters who struggle to maintain a loving relationship: Healing is possible. Last, but far from least, to God I say thank You for Your love, compassion, and consistency in my life. There is no greater love than Your love, God!

Tschanna Taylor

ONCE A FATHERLESS CHILD

Can you imagine what it's like to struggle to hold onto the one memory you have of your father? Well, I can because that is all I have left. I vaguely remember the tall, handsome man with the big afro. The man whom I would first love in my life was suddenly gone. All I ever wanted was what most little girls want: to be "Daddy's Little Girl." I will never have that, and that lost feeling as a little girl shaped the choices I made.

I'm not sure that as a child, we understand what death means. All we really know is that the person is gone and will never come back.

I was six years old when my mother came home and delivered the news that would change my life forever: My daddy was dead. At that moment, I couldn't describe what I felt. Now that I am older, I can put that feeling into words: I felt abandoned and lost. *Maybe if I had been a better child, God wouldn't have taken him from me. Why did my father have to leave? What was it about me that made it where he would never come back?* Those were the thoughts my young mind pondered over the years while growing up.

Anger began to set in as I watched my mother move on with her life. She married someone else about a month before my father died, and I was upset about that. Now, in my mind, I thought that *maybe* if she wouldn't have married this man, my father would still be alive. As time went on, my mother had two additional sons whom she raised. My parents were teenagers, so my grandmother raised me. Sometimes, I felt like a rejected child. There were moments in my life when I wondered why I wasn't wanted. As an adult, my mother and I had this conversation, and she informed me that she gave me a **choice**. Looking back, I often wondered, *"Why would she give me a* **choice***?"* I was only a child who was incapable of making adult decisions!

As a child, I spent a lot of time in my room writing in my journals about how I felt. Even surrounded by family, I felt alone. I can recall watching others with their dads, leaving me with the desire for just a piece of that. I longed for my dad daily and missed my mom being there like I thought a mother should be.

My grandmother gave me all the love in the world. At the time, it just wasn't enough. In our home, we didn't talk much about feelings—which I think is a big problem today. I was somehow supposed to be able to process all of this on my own. I honestly believe that Mu thought if she showed me enough love, I would be okay…but I wasn't. My paternal grandfather and uncles stepped in, doing their best to give me what I needed. Still, they just weren't my **DAD**! How could a person have so many people showing her so much love and still feel alone? Honestly, for me, it was watching those around me with their parents and thinking, *"Why can't that be* **ME***? Don't I deserve to have my parents here with* **ME***?"*

Having formed the thoughts of abandonment by my parents was the beginning of seeing myself as someone who didn't deserve to be loved. I felt worthless in so many ways. There was the feeling of being deserted by my father and God. I was raised to trust that God was always with me, but the thought of desertion broke my trust.

Little did I know that almost 20 years later, God would send me a spiritual father who would change all of that.

After struggling with the loss of my father all my life, I met Bishop L. Foday Farrar and everything changed. I recall the first time I saw this man when my best friend took me to her parents' house. Bishop Farrar was sitting in their front room as my friend, Sabrina, and I walked through the door. She introduced us, and he had this warm smile on his face. It was like I was home. *He later shared that when he saw me, he knew I was his spiritual daughter.*

During this time, I was still angry with the world and God because of the horrible things I had endured. Throughout my life, my anger with God had manifested in the worst way. Truthfully, I don't even think I realized just how angry I was until a conversation with my best friends led me to say it aloud. The moment I spoke it into the atmosphere was the moment some chains began to break in my life.

Bishop showed me the love of a father. I began to attend his church in 1996, where I stayed until I departed from Raleigh in 2014. No one could tell me that man was **NOT** my father! *LOL!* Sunday after Sunday, he imparted a word in my heart, but it was the moments outside the church that changed me. I had been cut in the face, raped, stabbed, and lost a child by this point and felt like God had abandoned me.

My relationship with God was damaged by my lack of trust, which Bishop helped me to restore.

Bishop Farrar was a man with so much love in his heart to share, and he did so unconditionally. He always made time to see me or take my calls. The Farrar family took me in as one of their own. I spent birthdays with them and even some holidays when I couldn't get back home to be with my family. Bishop was always straight with me, especially when I was in the wrong. The correction was always done in love. During my times of struggle, he made sure to let me know that I was special—not in a way that I was to think I was better than anyone else, but that God had a plan for my life. Bishop spoke over my life many times. There were moments when I thought, *"God can't use someone like me to bring change to others!"* Then, Bishop would tell me, *"Your struggles are not about you but the women you are called to help. Christina, do not sit on the gift God has given you. He has a plan for your life. Many are where you have been, and they need to know that they, too, can come out on the other side."* He also shared with me how he saw me reaching women all over the world. I thought to myself, **"That is a big responsibility. I'm not sure I can do that!"** He, however, had so much faith in me.

Then, in December 2015, I received a phone call that would change my life yet again. My friend, Michelle, called and when I answered, I knew something wasn't right just by the tone of her voice.

"Chris, I have something to tell you," Michelle said. *"Bishop is gone."*

My first response was, **"Gone where?"** I knew in my mind what she meant, but my heart just couldn't bear to face the truth. I thought, *"This must be a dream...well, more like a* **nightmare!**"

I fell to the floor, and all I could do was scream. My heart and mind were racing at the same time. *How could this be? Not Bishop Farrar! Not my spiritual father!* **Not again, Lord!**

When I went to view him, all I saw was **PEACE**, which put my heart at ease. Still, the pain of the loss was present. The great thing is that he gave me so much love and wisdom in 20 years. I will always have a part of him with me when I'm in a situation that would require his advice.

Bishop Farrar came into my life when I thought I would never be close to God. He taught me about relationships, which changed how I viewed everything around me. He showed me that a man doesn't have to be your biological father to love and be there for you. He listened to me when I needed help and never judged me. I realized our relationship with our fathers has a direct link to how we navigate our relationships with men and, more importantly, how we view our relationship with God. I never knew what it was like to be able to call on my biological father when I was in trouble, but later, I had the opportunity to experience that with Bishop. The love and trust he showed me helped me to open my heart to the love of God.

Bishop Farrar left an imprint on my heart that can never be removed.

I want to leave you with three tips on how to **heal**, be **equipped**, and get **restored** if you have experienced being a fatherless child:

1. **Heal** — Learn to love and trust who you are in the sight of God.
2. **Equip** — Strengthen your relationship with God daily and walk boldly into the destiny He has mapped out for you.
3. **Restore** — You are exactly who God says you are. Your past will not define your future results. God loves you through your mess into the masterpiece you will become.

CHRISTINA N SAUNDERS, CCLC

Christina Saunders is a Certified Christian Life Coach, Speaker and Advocate for domestic violence victims. Christina is known as Straight Talk Chris: The Restoration Coach. Her passion is to help women restore life after tragedy. As a conqueror of domestic violence, she is on a mission to show women that they can live a healthy and free life after abuse. She started her coaching business in 2014 which consist of one on one coaching and group coaching. Christina received her first certification as a Life Coach in October of 2014. Then she received a second certificate in May of 2017.

Christina is currently writing a book called *A Little Girl Broken* where she will share how losing her father at an early age set off a chain of events in her life that changed her forever. She also wrote a workbook called the *The 5 Steps to Breaking Soul Ties*. She is also a Co-Author of *H.E.R. Extreme Makeover: Reflections of Healing, Equipping and Restoring Messes to Masterpieces*.

Christina founded the Luv2BeYou Movement in 2018. Stay connected with Christina on social media at:

Facebook: www.facebook.com/straighttalkchris
Instagram: www.instagram.com/straighttalkchris
On the Web: www.straighttalkchris.com.

Erin Fuller-Russell

"Every time you thought you couldn't keep moving forward, you did. Take a moment to appreciate your strength."
~ Karen Salmonmsohn ~

Dedication

To my husband, Bobby: Thank you for loving and supporting me. To my children Eric, Briania, and Salia: One day you will understand the undeniable love a mother has for her children. To my mom, Jennifer: Thank you for raising me to be a strong woman of God. Most importantly, thank you, Jesus Christ, for loving me, even when I didn't know how to love myself.

Tschanna Taylor

BEAUTIFULLY BROKEN

"The Lord is close to the brokenhearted and saves those who are crushed in spirit..."
Psalms 34:18

I come from a family of ministers, dating back to my great-great-grandfather. He laid the foundation for my family and all the things he said that God promised him have come to fruition. *Would God keep His promises to me just as He did with my great-great-grandfather?*

Being 17 years old and not knowing what I wanted to do with my life after high school was one of the scariest moments of my life. I had no idea who I was or what I wanted to be. My life's path had not been crystal clear, and I had had my share of ups and downs. Growing up, I always felt like I was treated differently. Maybe the feeling was attributed to "Middle Child Syndrome." I don't know for sure, but what I did know with certainty is that I felt different. I was such a mess, but my mess began long before I was 17.

When I was ten years old, I was molested by my mother's boyfriend—the same man who later became her husband. They are still married today. *Yes, you read that right!*

At the age of 13, I was sexually assaulted and almost gang-raped by a group of neighborhood "friends."

When I was 14 years old, I entered into a relationship with a 21-year-old man.

In a span of only **four years**, my life had been turned upside down. There were things I was too young to precisely understand why they were happening to me at the time. I became a very angry and disrespectful teenager.

At the age of 17, I accepted my calling to become a minister. I was nowhere near ready. I couldn't even minister to *myself* at the time, but I knew the calling was placed on my life and could no longer deny it. *How could I help others when my own life was such a mess?* I was broken in so many ways. *Who would believe me?* Even though I knew the path my life was to take eventually, I wasn't sure why I was chosen when I was nowhere near qualified *(at least that's what I thought)*.

As I approached adulthood, my demons continued to follow and haunt me. I began to drink heavily and experimented with marijuana and pills. The hurt of my past was consuming my life. Alcohol and drugs caused me to blame others for my behavior. I thought that was part of my healing process. I was partying and hanging out with people I knew I shouldn't have been around. I thought I was getting rid of the hurt and shame by trying to be someone I wasn't. I had so much hatred in my heart for virtually everyone, especially those who were close to me as a child.

How could they let so much hurt happen to me? Did they not see or even notice my pain? **Did they not care?**

One day, I prayed to God and begged Him to take away the pain. I couldn't take it anymore. The pain had consumed my life long enough, and I was done. It hit me like a ton of bricks, and I could no longer fight this thing alone. I took a long look in the mirror and decided that the trauma of my past would not overshadow the triumphs of my future. At that moment, I began to take back my life.

I had to learn how to forgive. I had to learn what true forgiveness was. I had heard so many times that forgiveness is for me and not the other person. I never really understood what that meant until I was faced with having to forgive the people who hurt me. Now, this miraculous transformation did not happen overnight. It took years of counseling, prayer, crying, and most of all, learning how to forgive myself because of all the self-blaming. I felt like I had done something to make those people hurt me. I always said, *"If I had or hadn't done 'this or that,' then maybe "it" wouldn't have happened."*

The truth is this: It *HAD* to happen.

Do I think God meant to hurt or harm me? **NO!** Do I believe He allowed certain things to happen in my life to help define me? **YES!**

Forgiveness gave me strength. It gave me the will to give up alcohol and drugs. It gave me a love for myself that I never knew I had. Forgiveness gave me **FREEDOM!** I was no longer ashamed to talk about the molestation and the fact that the person is still a part of my everyday life. It doesn't bother me. I can now have a decent conversation with that person and love him with the love of God. Forgiveness allowed me to be free of the fear of what others would think of me. Forgiveness allowed me to walk in my calling.

Being able to share my testimony of no longer being bound by hurt and pain has allowed me to help other women. A lot of times, people choose not to forgive because they think it gives the other person a pass. True forgiveness means that for me to move forward and be happy in my life, I have to let go of the anger that consumes me. Sometimes, forgiveness will have to take place without an apology — and that is okay, too.

Forgive so that you can be set free!

I thought the pieces of my broken past would no longer fit together again. The beauty of broken pieces is that you get to put them back together again, piece by piece, carefully and lovingly until they become the masterpiece you think it should be.

ERIN FULLER-RUSSELL

Erin Fuller-Russell was born and raised in the small town of Griffin, Georgia, located just outside of Atlanta. She is the Owner of EBS Enterprise and has made it her personal goal to educate as many people as possible on the physical and spiritual benefits of forgiveness and healing.

In January 2018, Erin launched the "Broken but Chosen" Tour. She uses this platform to not only speak of her personal experiences, but to also open a dialogue for others who may think they are alone. Before embarking on this journey of writing for *H.E.R. Extreme Makeover*, Erin spent most of her adult life working and spending time with her family.

Erin is married to Bobby Russell and together, they have six children. They currently reside in Clemmons, North Carolina.

Facebook: @Broken-But-Chosen-400698433808100
Email: brokenbutchosen@gmail.com

Tina L. Moore

"What seems to us as bitter trials are often blessings in disguise."
~ Oscar Wilde ~

Dedication

To my love, Kevin Burton: Thank you for standing by my side. I appreciate you and us so much. To my children and grandchildren: Stay focused and dream big. It's never too late to accomplish your goals. To my mother: I truly appreciate all that you do. Lastly, to my grandparents: Continue to rest in Heavenly peace.

FROM BITTER TO BLESSED

As an only child, there were many times when I **hated** my life. It was just my mother and me, leaving me very envious of my cousins because they had *both* of their parents in the home. I had no one to talk to or share my most intimate feelings with. Many days, I talked to myself, but where do the real answers come from? I wasn't comfortable with talking to my mother or any other family member, so I kept a lot bottled up inside. My childhood was what it was.

I have a big family and spent a lot of time with my grandparents and cousins. Growing up with them was an absolute joy, especially when considering I was an only child. There were sleepovers just about every weekend because my mother would hang out with her brothers and whichever sibling's house was the meetup spot at the time is where all the kids stayed. For me, some homes were better to stay at than others. In stark contrast, my cousins always seemed comfortable no matter where they were. In the beginning, I didn't care either.

Then came a time when I did care...

There was one particular home I grew to resent visiting. No one was around to protect me from the evilness of a child molester. I often questioned why my cousins allowed the molestation to happen to me. Why did my **mother** allow it to happen? Why did that family member choose **ME** to violate? At the tender age of around eight or nine, what could I have done to deserve to be touched and mishandled the way that I was? What was it about me that caused that family member to destroy mind and body, all while telling me he didn't want to hurt me if only he could keep "it" right there? He would warn me to not say anything about what he had done because if I did, I would be the reason the family would no longer have get-togethers. Being young and unaware, I believed him. I absolutely loved my family and did not want to be the reason my mother and her brothers didn't partake in their weekend rituals of family fun.

I am grateful to God that there was only one instance of molestation with that family member, but there were other sleepover nights in my pre-teen years when I was awakened out of my sleep by his hand touching me in ways I shouldn't have been. I wanted him to stop bothering me. I hated his touch and refused to allow him to keep doing ungodly things to me. When I finally gained the nerve one night to tell him to leave me alone, I closed my eyes tightly and said, *"I'm telling, and I'm going to tell **right now**."* After saying that, he hauled tail away from me and never touched me again.

As a teenager, I was timid, and my self-esteem was the lowest of the low. There was so much from my past that I blocked out. I was numb to the pain. I always felt there was something weird about me. It didn't even matter to me if I didn't do those things that normal teens did. I wasn't active in anything while in high school and didn't attend college until later in my adult life. I wasn't a fashionista with trendy, cute clothes and shoes. I was "average" and never felt the *need* to fit in. I had no desire to dream, aspire to become someone significant, or even focus on my future. If anything, I was lost and unaware of the bitterness that lied ahead.

I wasn't a social butterfly and preferred that boys didn't talk to me at all. There was a time I had the strangest relationship ever, though. I laugh about it today and, after seeing my ex-boyfriend for the first time in years, it brought up a flood of memories of our time together. My shyness as a teenager remained with me, even after the birth of my first child. I wasn't in a relationship with her father, but he was someone who had shown some interest in me. It was a sexual interest, but an interest nonetheless. After the birth of my daughter, he became a part of our lives. I believed he was someone who could love me. Lo and behold, *that* fantasy was short-lived. I became a victim of domestic violence on an almost daily basis.

The lowest of the low came when he locked my daughter and me out of our apartment because he was inside getting high on crack cocaine. When he finally let us in, he blew the smoke in my face. I decided right then and there that I was done and left him for good. Leaving him didn't end the abuse. I ended up having another child and things were quite rocky, but I thank God for my mother and grandmother's support.

For some time, my bitterness lingered, but it had a happy face that masked it. I can't put into words how that looks, but I knew in my heart that something good was waiting for me.

A few years later, I met someone who I thought was the man of my dreams. A year after we met, we married. To say the least, we had a cute, little family. I had my third child and, again, believed this relationship was to be my "happily ever after." This time, however, it came with alcohol and drug use without physical abuse. Once that part of my life was over, I began to clearly see the roots of my bitterness and depression.

Feeling like such a failure at life, I turned to alcohol on a daily basis. Being a bartender probably caused me more harm than good. Even though the money was excellent and I had men eating out of the palm of my hands, I had no regard for others; it was all about me, what I wanted, and what I was going to get. I was all about getting money…*and that next drink.* There were a few times when I don't know how I made it home after a night of hanging out in the bar and after-hour joint.

Bitterness and depression were toxic companions. I made up my mind that the life I was living was **NOT** the life I wanted to live. I knew my choice of lifestyle wasn't in God's plan. It wasn't my *purpose.* I knew I was called to do and be more. I began to pray and pray for a better outcome. I asked God to show me and lead me in the direction to be there for people in a **positive** way. I desired to be proud of whatever path God would direct me. It was then that He told me to think about something beneficial to my youngest daughter and oldest granddaughter. I was then given the inspiration to start an etiquette school for girls. Later, the vision broadened and God directed me to give back to both girls **and** young women *(when you educate a girl, you educate a nation and we can all grow daily in our personal development and self-improvement).*

I think of my grandmother often. I recall how she prayed about **everything**. I promise you this: There is **not one** person alive today who can outmatch the kindhearted soul of the woman whom I loved dearly.

Today, when I am faced with trials and tribulations, I talk to God about them and also ask: "**WWGD?** *(What would Grumma do?)*" In August 2017, I gave my life to Christ. For me, that was the best decision I could have ever made. My heart is filled with loving the Lord, and I thank Him every day for bringing me out of so many storms. I am free, at peace, and will forever be grateful to God for never giving up on me.

My bitterness has changed to blessings, and I am mighty proud to share my joys!

I leave you with the following three tips on how you can **HEAL**, be **EQUIPPED**, and get **RESTORED**:

1. To *Heal* in any situation:
    a. Be yourself.
    b. Know your worth.
    c. Be specific in your wants.
2. How to *Equip*:
    a. Keep God first.
    b. Live courageously in your everyday life.
    c. Practice kindness at all times.
3. How to *Restore*:
    a. Find out and understand what being spiritual is.
    b. Reconnect with God.
    c. Let go of anger.

"She is clothed with strength and dignity, and she laughs without fear of the future."
~ Proverbs 31:25 ~

TINA L. MOORE

Tina L. Moore is a Self-Confidence/Self-Esteem Mentor for girls, Personal Development Strategist for young adult women, and Co-Author of *H.E.R. Extreme Makeover: Reflections of Healing, Equipping, and Restoring Messes into Masterpieces*. She is the Owner of Everlasting Impressions Candy Bouquets and Gift Baskets, Personally Yours Concierge/Errand Service, Yellow Rubies Mentoring Program for Girls, The Yellow Apron Meal Preparation, Just Me and My Bucket Residential Cleaning Service, TDK Online Boutique, and is the Founder of Sister Action Social Group.

Tina is the mother of four phenomenal children: Shayla, Jeremy, Michael, and Divad. She's 'Meema' to five wonderfully made grandchildren: Kyair, Harlem, Jymere, Jahsier, and Ger'nee.

Tina's educational background includes an Applied Science Associate's Degree in Medical Assisting and Medical Insurance Billing & Coding. She also holds Certification as a Medical Assistant.

She also serves on the Hospitality Ministry Board at her church, Antioch Missionary Baptist Church in Rochester, New York.

Facebook: @yellowgazelle18
Facebook: @TDK-Boutique-312471439403969
Email: tinalmoore08@gmail.com

Kier Ayers

"Nothing is impossible. The word itself says 'I'm possible'."
~ Audrey Hepburn ~

Dedication
To my first loves, children and baby loves, and grandchildren: I love you with everything in me. Thank you for being a constant source of inspiration. You are the reason I strive to accomplish every goal. I love you all!

I Mastered the Art of Hiding

Here it is...another day. Much like the days before, it started with lies and denials. I lived in a make-believe fantasy world of peaches and cream, hiding so no one could see how deeply-depressed I was. *"I'm doing well,"* was my unwavering response—no matter how I felt. I had developed the ability to both cover and manipulate myself and others over the years regarding the feelings I had. Learning to cover up what needed to be purged and not confronting anything concerning my true feelings proved to destroy everything that could have been a light in my life.

After the tears dried and a day was taken to gather my thoughts concerning my failed marriage, I came face-to-face with myself for the first time in life. What I saw was not at all what I expected: a woman, mother, and grandmother who had countless sessions with others about everything from depression to single-parenting to love and even the basics of living life. I couldn't bear to see what I had become due to never being taught the necessity of loving oneself. **Whew! Could it be true?** Facing the fact that self-love was not a part of my daily life was scary. Going through the process of learning how to love myself was even more frightening.

What I learned in that very instant was that I had not allowed the God I served wholeheartedly to have complete control of my life. I had to dig deep and challenge myself to unearth those dead things that kept me bound in order to live a life that was fulfilling, healthy, and glorified God.

Now, the struggle begins...

Sleepless nights. Restless days. No peace or happiness for days on end. The loss of a job and home.

After all I had been through, I still couldn't bring myself to see me and the real problem in the mirror. Not taking ownership and responsibility for my own happiness was delaying the process of healing that the Lord was trying to take me through. I cried a few more days, fought against myself a little more, allowed alcohol to become my comforter, and secluded myself from those who loved me. One day, rock bottom became my portion. I just couldn't handle it another day. Thoughts of suicide invaded my mind for the first time ever. You see, suicide would have been an easy way out, but the way I'm made up would not allow for that option to become my reality. No matter my circumstance, I could not let people see me in that light. Not many knew I was dying a slow death. I couldn't let them find out that my marriage had fallen apart, that depression had a death grip on me, and that I had become a borderline alcoholic.

Hiding had become my specialty, and I knew I had mastered it.

The self-exploration process began. Growing in self-love has proven to be the most liberating and life-altering experience I've ever had. See, placing blame on another person is easy, but becoming strong enough to face yourself and the real issues in the midst of obstacles in the way forces you to develop strength, birth wisdom and results in a transformation that **only God** can foster.

As I steadied myself for what was ahead, digging deep meant going back further than my failed marriage, single parenthood, or even church hurt. It meant facing a terrible pain that blinded my eyes and held me back. It meant forgiving a man who left me (in my opinion) to fend for myself and prompted me to build a wall of fear around me that caused me to need to control what only God should have the power to control.

Self-control is one thing, but it set me up for failure in every relationship to come. As I made an effort daily to heal and be honest with myself, the mirror became a little easier to look into. Although I found myself still hiding from others, I was no longer hidden from myself. I rebuilt my prayer life, restructured my family life, and began to accept the fact that I could not change what once was. I could only be responsible for what was in the present moment: myself.

I had no control over parents who abandoned me, the person who molested me, the drugs that plagued my family, nor any other thing life threw at me to make me doubt my calling and purpose. I could only build and resolve to take life one day at a time and truly release my life to God, allowing His healing and transforming power to control my everyday existence.

The transforming and restorative power of God healed my broken heart and renewed my mind while building me up for this season of my life. Had that particular pain not broken me down, I may have never realized that I needed to be rebuilt. I now see life in a completely different way. The struggles I once had for self-love are no more. The inability to say *"NO!"* to toxic and negative energy is nonexistent. My days are no longer governed by the quest to prove to others that **I am enough**. My daily messes have become a part of the flawless masterpiece my Heavenly Father is growing me to be. I am **healed, delivered**, and **growing** in the power of His love. ***Wow!*** I am new and, for the first time in my life, I make no apologies for my beauty. I've arrived, and this self-love will forever be worth fighting for.

As you have read my story, I pray *something* written has given a little insight on how to move past the break in your life and rebuild the link that connects you to our Father. As it is with any fight, knowing the real enemy is imperative. First, acknowledge the issue and face it head-on. Facing it doesn't make you weak. Rather, it slowly prepares you to fight the battle that is soon to come. Once you face it, you will be able to equip yourself for that battle. It may sometimes take prayer, fasting, speaking affirmations, or partnering with others to gain strength. Each fight is unique and will require different equipment. During a battle, know that the enemy of your soul is playing for keeps.

We must do the same, with purpose and without apology. Guard yourself, protect your heart, and preserve your healing. You're worth it!

Always pray for direction on who can cover you during those moments of weakness. When necessary, remove yourself from the situation until you have the strength to take another step in your process. Affirm yourself daily. Be it with quotes or scriptures, do something **every single day** that will build you up and help keep you focused. Surround yourself with people who are strong enough to carry you while you are transitioning. Allow **no** negative energy into your space while you heal.

Healing is an opportunity to rebuild what was once broken or to build anew. Either way, accept the process, make the necessary changes, and do whatever it takes to be your best self. *Grow and Glow, my friend!* God would have it no other way!

KIER AYERS

Kier Ayers was born and raised in Jersey City, New Jersey. As a teenage mom, she faced many obstacles in her young life. Her tenacity and faith in God helped her persevere. Today, she is a true servant whose heart is filled with compassion to help continue building the masses.

Kier (a.k.a. 'Chef Journey' and Owner of "The Journey Co.") believes both prayer and food always make things better. She received her Culinary, Hospitality, and Natural Hair Care Certifications from Wake Technical Community College. She is a co-author of the book *Bag Ladies Unpacked*.

She is a mom of two and a grandmother of five who enjoys crocheting, sewing, singing, and spending quality time with family and friends.

Email: legacycc75@gmail.com
Instagram: @legacycateringconfections
Facebook: @experiencethejourney
Facebook: @legacycateringconfections

Tschanna Taylor

Shanae Starnes

"Surely goodness and mercy shall follow me all the days of my life, and I will dwell in the house of the Lord forever."
~ Psalms 23:6 ~

Dedication
To my best friend and love, LeWarren Jackson, and our three beautiful children, Nakiya, Jahmia, and LeWarren, Jr.: I appreciate you for allowing me the time to complete such an endearing project. Thank you to my parents, Tony and Jackie Neely, for your constant support. Sincere gratitude is also given to my grandmother, Quincy Starnes, for always lending your listening ear and constant support.

Tschanna Taylor

The Journey of My Voice's Revival

It was the morning of July 18, 2016. I awoke saddened and with a heavy heart. It was a day full of sunshine, with not a whistle from the wind. I recall my thoughts running through my mind like a motion picture of the days prior to when I last saw my friend. This day will never be the same for me...

Our relationship started in 1992. She was my mom's hairstylist, who became my hairstylist and then mentor when I began Cosmetology school in 1996. As time progressed, she and I both became Cosmetology teachers. I kept in touch with her and leaned on her for wisdom. To learn that my friend and mentor of 24 years suddenly passed away from a stroke left me in a state of total shock and disbelief. I was under the impression that she was doing well after recovering from a previous stroke. My friend was special to so many people. Her passing left a void in my heart, but it also encouraged me to focus on my health.

On July 19th, I made a doctor's appointment to get myself checked. My friend's passing had that great of an impact on me. I even started noticing slight pressure under my left breast. At the conclusion of the doctor's exam, she asked, *"Have you ever had an EKG performed?"* The question initially startled me, and then I replied, *"Well, no. I never had to have one done before."* The doctor went on to explain what an EKG was (an EKG is a paper or digital recording of the electrical signals in the heart, also referred to as an electrocardiogram or ECG), why it was necessary to have one, and how the procedure was done. It didn't take long for the EKG to complete in the office on that day. All sorts of emotions flooded in. I was scared, nervous, anxious...and fearful.

It didn't help decrease my fear when the doctor returned and used a soft, quiet tone to explain the EKG results. My heart sank once she explained there was a blockage on the left bundle branch of my heart. This type of obstruction makes the heart pump harder to allow blood to flow efficiently through the circulatory system. After the doctor shared that news, she scheduled an appointment with a Cardiologist, all while assuring me I shouldn't worry.

Even though she asserted that I would be alright, I was scared and hurt. Tears started rolling down my face as she tried to console me. All I could hear were the words *"heart"* and *"blockage"* echoing through my mind. I felt weak. I felt perishable. It was bad...

It was 7:00 a.m. on July 20, 2016, when I suddenly noticed a sharp pain under my left breast as I was preparing for the day. The pain was slight but noticeable. As I inhaled deeply, the feeling came again. It was subtle but definitely present. With all that had happened, my head felt heavy. I was sweating like I had run a three-mile course. My body felt tired. Above all else, the most painful thing was the mounting fear of having a stroke or heart attack. Various thoughts crossed my mind. Some were intense, ushering in the onset of a panic attack. I somehow gathered my strength and drove myself to the nearest emergency room: Carolina Medical Center.

Fortunately, there weren't many patients at that time, so I was able to meet with the General Physician quickly. By this time, however, I felt somewhat better. *Maybe it was the thought that I made it safely to the hospital that made me feel better...*

When my turn arrived, a fleet of thoughts ran through my mind. I hoped the prognosis wasn't bad, but I was nervous. I was kept overnight and given a battery of tests. The next day when the doctor came in, he was warm and pleasant. He patiently listened to all I had to say. After quietly listening to me, he asked me if I had ever used hard drugs before. I replied, *"No."* He then informed me I had an enlarged heart and diagnosed me with Congestive Heart Failure (a condition that means the heart is weak and can lead to a dangerous build-up of fluids due to the circulatory dysfunction).

Two weeks later, I was preparing for my 3:00 p.m. appointment with the Cardiologist. I was at home thinking about what the emergency room doctor told me. It wasn't easy to absorb his official diagnosis. As a matter-of-fact, it was outright frightening and threatening. The more I thought about it, the more I cried.

I started accusing God. I questioned Him: *"Why, Lord? Why **ME**? What have I done to deserve all of this? Have I hurt You? Have I done something wrong? Have You left Your hopes in me? Why???"* Hot tears fell from my eyes as I spoke those words. My heart was breaking. I felt betrayed. I felt completely abandoned. I accused Him of **everything**.

After all of those accusations against God, I felt *worse*.

I knew blaming Him wasn't going to help, but I didn't know what else to do. Life seemed hopeless to me. Life was being unjust. Life didn't care about me anymore. The thoughts were driving me crazy! Slowly, I succumbed to depression. I lost hope and felt fragile and forlorn. Time seemed to rush by faster than ever. It appeared death wanted a face-to-face encounter with me. Blood was rushing through my veins. My brain felt like it was about to explode under the pressure. I felt very defeated. I just knew my time had come to an end.

Abruptly, the face of my son flashed before my eyes. Then, the faces of my daughters and all those who loved me joined the vision. All of them needed me in their lives. All of those faces were supported by my existence. Out of nowhere, I heard a voice that silenced my fears and anxieties. It was a compelling voice that touched my heart and calmed me on the inside. That voice healed me when it said:

"Listen, Shanae. You are wonderful. Don't you remember the days that have passed by when you were riddled with grief about the loss of your grandfather, whom you loved as a father and who raised you as his own? Don't you recall the bad things that have happened to you as a promiscuous teenager? Did you forget all the crises you faced before? Shanae, this is no different from the others. Remember how brave you were in those moments of trouble? Remember how you refused to give up? Remember when nothing was strong enough to stop you? Why have you given up your hopes now? Why do you look defeated? Many lives are looking up to you for their wellbeing. They need you. They love you. You have three beautiful children whom you have brought up in love and care. They can never imagine their lives without you. You are precious to them, just as you are to many others. Above all else, you are strong. Nothing can stop you from what you

should be — except you. If you give up, you lose. If you lose, the people who love you lose. And if they lose, your life will be meaningless. Shanae, learn from your past. Try to remember how you had developed the courage and bravery required in those moments. Life is the best teacher. Learn from it, for this moment requires the same. So, forget your fears and pains. Take proper actions. As for the problem, you will overcome if you stay strong. As for me, I am your inner-voice which was being suppressed by your fears."

I was amazed by all I had heard. That voice energized me and gave me back the voice I thought was lost! I knew this was not my end. My journey was not over. I had to live more and live for others. My fears started to diminish. **But *GOD*!**

At 3:00 p.m., as I sat in the Cardiologist's office, I wondered whether all of this happened because of me or was it just one of those times for a valuable lesson to be learned? The meeting with the Cardiologist went surprisingly well. I realized that *time* was needed to mend me back together again. The Cardiologist told me that modern-day science was a miracle in and of itself and that I could recover without any surgeries by following some strict routines. The Cardiologist was quite meek but humorous and mood-elevating, allowing me to finally realize that our lives depend on how we respond to life and that to deal with any crisis, we must have a positive attitude.

It is now 2019. Life has changed a lot for me since then. I have made it a point to continue adhering to the routine that the Cardiologist suggested and get through it, regardless of any obstacles that may come. Indeed, with time, I've gotten healthier.

Sometimes, crises are good. They help to revive the inner-voice that teaches life's most important lessons and helps us begin to reason. That same inner-voice sustains us in ways that enable us to move forward in peace.

My voice has intercepted thoughts of giving up and replaced them with a voice of resilience.

I leave with you the following three points that will help you be **healed**, **equipped**, and **restored** on your journey with your own inner-voice:

- ❖ *Visualize a solution.* — Your vision is pertinent to your survival. Imagine a solution for things to work out well while being intentional about creating a new approach and perspective.
- ❖ *Reflect on how you overcame past situations.* — Realize that God has continued to equip you. Count it all joy and work towards your healing again.
- ❖ *Forgive yourself and keep pushing forward.* —Press on and handle life's difficulties by seeing them as God's masterpiece, which is a powerful way to experience His grace and mercy.

SHANAE STARNES, BBA, MA Ed.

Shanae Starnes, BBA, MA Ed., known as the "Inspirational Motivator" is an Author, Financial Literacy Consultant, Entrepreneur, Mother, and Cosmetology Career and Technical Educator living her dreams.

Shenae is the Co-Author of *H.E.R. Extreme Makeover: Reflections of Healing, Equipping and Restoring Messes into Masterpieces*, and shares her story about resilience and faith. In her book, *Keeping Score*, Shanae shows and encourages others on how to better handle their credit which, in turn. helps people improve their finances. Manifesting one's financial literacy has been her focus since 2013 when she began her tax preparation business "Ideal Tax and Bookkeeping, Inc." Her company also assists with creating budgets, credit education/restoration, asset protection through health and life insurance, and financial literacy.

For more information, email starnesshanae@gmail.com.

Facebook: @sstarnes1
Instagram: @shanaestarnes
Twitter: @shanaedastylist
LinkedIn: linkedin.com/in/Shanae-starnes-215a05100

Angela Chance

"The world as we have created it is a process of our thinking. It cannot be changed without changing our thinking."
~ Albert Einstein ~

Dedication

I dedicate this story to my mother, **Josephine Chance**, my earthly example of God's unconditional love, mercy, forgiveness, kindness, and emotional stability. As well, this is for all the women who struggle with emotional health issues and are embarking on their journey of being healed, equipped, and restored back to wholeness on three levels.

From Depression to Deliverance

In the African-American community, the mental health system is not designed to provide the best health care. In my experience, neither is the church. Imagine if these two systems weren't against each other. Envision them working side-by-side to help in the healing process for Black women. With the two systems working together, the services provided would free many African-American women who suffer from the **"Strong, Black Woman Syndrome."** According to the National Alliance on Mental Illness, African-American women are less likely to seek mental health care for emotional issues — more than any other race of people.

At first, I didn't seek professional or spiritual help because I didn't feel safe enough to be totally honest about my mental and emotional state. Family, friends, and the church unintentionally made me feel as if I either didn't have enough faith in God or was being too "dramatic."

Healing starts from a place of honesty.

I have always believed that if I could be 100% honest, I could find all kinds of doors to God's healing. I remember trying to seek help in the mental and spiritual arenas. Like most adults, I have experienced trauma from people, situations, and circumstances. Finding support was a different type of trauma within itself in the Black community. What is most harmful is the lack of knowledge and not being adequately equipped to handle the difficult parts of life.

I was a Black woman trying to stay afloat in a sea of "isms." Rac**ISM**, sex**ISM**, and class**ISM**—coupled with exposure to violence and lack of community and family support—has prejudicially perpetrated upon the psyche of the Black woman. I was not excluded from what is common to all of us: injustices, hard places, loss, and no healing. These factors have set the stage for me to raise my children while being mentally and emotionally unstable. I look back over the years of being a mother and realize I raised four beautiful children while battling emotional and mental issues that I (nor anyone else) recognized or understood. I was extremely shocked when I was diagnosed with Post-Traumatic Stress Disorder (PTSD) in 2013. Prior to that, I had been diagnosed with depression in 1990 and an anxiety disorder in 2000. PTSD was not a topic of discussion back then, but as I reflect on the traumas of my life, I was actually a perfect candidate for PTSD. I believe many Black women unknowingly suffer with mental/emotional issues, but much like me, the stigma associated with mental health causes us to push our mental health aside, hide behind a mask, and don our best poker face.

My emotional traumas started in childhood. I realized that abandonment and rejection had slowly invaded who I was. As I grew from a child to a teen and finally to adulthood, negative beliefs and self-doubt grew as well. My mother was intentional with never talking bad about my father. She allowed me to form my own opinions concerning him when I got older. *I often wondered why I didn't have a dad and thought every kid had a father…except me.* Later in life, I realized not everyone had a father, but for so long (from my perspective), I was the **only** one. I was no man's "Princess." My father never came around, causing me to believe it was my fault that he wasn't there. In my undeveloped mind, I reasoned that since my mother never spoke poorly about him, who else could be at fault but me? I never blamed my mother because at that time in my life, I thought she could do no wrong, was the best mother ever, and she was my hero.

Fast-forward to my teenage years. My thoughts toward my mother turned the opposite. I was disrespectful, mean, and bratty. *Years later, my mother would say that at the age of 15, I went to sleep as her little girl and woke up unrecognizable.* I became rebellious and judgmental. I began to blame her for everything wrong in my life—including my father ignoring the fact that I existed and him not caring about my wellbeing. In my mind, my mother became the enemy.

Abandonment and rejection had slowly and successfully changed my mindset. Those negative energies integrated with my positive beliefs and emotions, confusing my immature mind. Childhood, teenage, and adult issues led me to many avoidable problems and traumas in my life that shaped my inner-thoughts. Internally, the storm of the century was brewing, and it manifested in my external life. My negative thoughts and outlook affected my physical, financial, and societal life.

Lack of knowledge in the church and fear of judgment from family and friends must be addressed within our community. We often concentrate on the fact that God heals, but it seems only to apply to the physical body. *Is therapy taboo in the church?* I ask that question because I recall one of the many dark times in my life, when I was very faithful in my church with attendance and money, believing in God, and striving to live a life pleasing to Him, yet I was not being pulled out of the darkness. The stress of single motherhood, the daily drudge of working, and doing "mommy things," along with the pain of my emotions were overwhelming. I was smiling when I should have been crying. I was holding in my pain when I should have been shouting about it from the rooftop. I was saying "YES!" when I should have been saying "NO!" All at once, it all came crashing down on me. I purposed in my heart one night that at church, I would reach out for help.

I was tired of being in pain.

I was tired of being confused.

I was tired of being solely responsible for my four children and me.

I was tired of *pretending*.

I needed some help!

That night at church, when they asked if anyone wanted to come to the altar to pray, I **JUMPED** out of my seat and **RAN** to the front. I threw myself on the altar. I cried to the Lord and didn't care who heard me. I needed healing in my mind. I confessed to God how tired I was and that I didn't want to be a mother anymore. The women of the church gathered around me, rubbed my back, and whispered, *"That's right; cry out to the Lord."* Yes, you read that correctly: I said I did not want to be a mother anymore. I was in a dark place and hurting in my very soul. I didn't know any other way to express myself at that moment.

No one from the church—leaders nor lay people—followed up with me to see if I was okay. **No one** suggested spiritual or professional mental health counseling. I don't blame them for not recognizing I needed both prayer *AND* therapy. I struggled for many years dealing with pain and darkness, trying to be a "good Christian."

I must pause here and provide some additional background so that you further understand the depths of my darkness and depression:

I was diagnosed with Alopecia Areata—an autoimmune disease that caused me to have patchy, bald spots all over my head. In addition, I also received a diagnosis of having Squamous Carcinoma Skin Cancer, a 10% hearing loss, **AND** my hormones were depleting because of the onset of menopause that caused sleepless nights, hot flashes, and weight gain. The depressive state I was in was **REAL**! I could not see my way out and was left to feel like this was my permanent state. I didn't like any of it one bit.

My previous spiritual experience may have caused me to question if therapy was taboo in the church, but I never lost my faith in God. I decided to take control of my own life and asked the dermatologist to refer me to a psychiatrist. I was not coping well with the diagnoses. I knew I needed to be accountable for my life by seeking the help needed for my healing and deliverance. I started to reason within myself that seeking therapy was not an indication of a lack of faith or disbelief in God. Family and friends said things like, *"Oh, suck it up!"* and *"You're just sad. It'll go away,"* and *"There's nothing wrong with you."* Each statement invalidated my feelings and devalued me as a person.

The mental health field and spiritual community failed me.

This time, I wouldn't fail myself.

I recognized that I was broken. I sought medical help for my *physical* needs, so why not do the same for my *mental* wellbeing?

To get from a place of **"Depression to Deliverance,"** I applied three steps that took me through the healing process. I still apply the same three principles in every area of my life today. I call it the "3-T Method":

Heal. Equip. Restore. My "3-T Method"
(Time, Thoughts, and Trust) for you:

HEALING: I had to be honest with myself and come to grips with the fact that it was going to take *TIME*; my healing wouldn't be immediate.

EQUIPPING myself with tools, the Word of God, and always being aware of my *THOUGHTS*.

RESTORED to the woman God created me to be, full of peace and purpose. I had to *TRUST* God and not lean unto my own understanding.

A setback is **not** an indication that you aren't healed. Situations and circumstances sometimes come just to show you how far you've come on your journey to personal peace and purpose.

~~~~~~~~~~

Angela Chance (a.k.a. Miss IQ (Information Queen)) is a Co-Author of *H.E.R. Extreme Makeover: Reflections of Healing, Equipping, and Restoring Messes Into Masterpieces*, Community Organizer, Legislative Liaison, Mental Health Advocate, Entrepreneur, and Health/Wellness Coach. She founded From Alopecia to Afro, Rock Your 'Fro Day, and the 3-Level Health Organization that supports and advocates for health physically, mentally, and emotionally, all while encouraging women to heal from the inside out and to include mental and emotional health in their permanent self-care routine.

Email: archance@gmail.com

Nakisha D. Blackwell

"For I know the plans I have for you," declares the LORD, "plans to prosper you and not to harm you, plans to give you hope and a future."
~ Jeremiah 29:11 ~

Dedication
I dedicate this story to God, my Spiritual Father, Provider, and Protector. I also dedicate this story to my children Ashlei, Rashid, and Jalon — my three hearts. I will always love you unconditionally.

Tschanna Taylor

ONCE BROKEN; NOW HEALED!

I was thrilled to have finally arrived at our destination…just he and I. It was a moment I had longed for: a stroll on the beach. The warm winds were briskly blowing through my hair, and the sounds of the waves rushing on the shore were relaxing. As we slowly walked along the beach, laughing and enjoying each other's presence, it was that special moment that grasped my attention; the moment of silence. We had a great friendship and had been exclusively dating for a while. We were each other's best friend. He turned to me with "that look" in his eyes—the look that said, "I don't want to live life without you." He tenderly kissed my forehead and then wrapped me in his arms. At that moment, I felt an embracing of both warmth and peace envelop me. That was the moment I knew…

Pretty much, that's almost every girl's dream…marrying their best *friend (at least that was **my** dream)*. I'm sure I'm not the only woman who, during her teenage years, used to daydream about how life would be. From the first date to walking down the aisle to finally be united with my king, I had it **ALL** meticulously planned out. I was going to be a phenomenal wife and mother. *(Notice I said I had it all planned out.)* Unfortunately, my plan was not God's plan.

"For I know the plans I have for you," says the Lord. "They are plans for good and not for disaster, to give you a future and a hope."
~ **Jeremiah 29:11, NLT** ~

It was not in **MY** plan to have cancer. It was not in **MY** plan to have my left thyroid removed. Still, I believe God will often allow our plans to follow through to the end so that **HE** will get the glory.

I grew up without my father. Often, I wondered how it would feel to be a "Daddy's Girl" — one protected by her father's love. Perhaps some of my choices in men would have been wiser were my father around. I was "that girl" who ended up seeking attention to fill a void. Something was missing, leaving me feeling incomplete. I ended up getting pregnant at the age of 17 and gave birth two weeks after my 18th birthday. Then, three years later (at the age of 21), I was married. Fourteen years later, I was divorced.

So, you see, I had it all planned out well — except for the part about the divorce. I don't think anyone who makes it to the altar has plans for the marriage to end in divorce. *Why did I still feel incomplete?* Even after my divorce, I seemed to attract unhealthy and toxic friendships and relationships. I started to question, *"What was I doing wrong?"* and *"Why did this have to happen to me?"* I was a "good woman" with a "good heart," but I was **also** a woman with a tongue that was sharp as a knife if you crossed me the wrong way. I started to force that "I'm a good woman" scenario on everyone, instead of allowing them to realize it on their own. As well, I quickly got caught up in my emotions. All I wanted was someone to love me just as much as I loved them.

What I didn't understand was why the word *LOVE* was often loosely used. If *LOVE* is defined as a strong feeling of affection, then why does *LOVE* sometimes cause us to feel **pain**?

After dealing with toxic relationships and friendships, I realized I had become a bitter woman. You know the kind; resentful of the *world* because of bad experiences. I was angry inside but kept it hidden. I was always great at covering up the mess. I started having trust issues, whether it was dealing with a friendship or romantic relationship. At one point, I was a broken and lost woman. I began to blame myself for the things that happened instead of seeing the fault in what someone did to me.

> *Wait. How could this be?*
> *I was a strong woman who was now broken?*
> *How did that happen? More importantly,*
> **WHY** *did I allow this to happen to* **ME**?
> *Could it be that men were able to see my brokenness?*

Yes, I said it. I was a broken woman, but my healing did not come from admitting my brokenness. Acceptance was the first part of the process. I recall the day I had grown tired of it all. I was physically, mentally, and spiritually exhausted. I remember that day like it was yesterday…

I literally fell to the floor, tears flowing heavily down my face. I started crying out to God. I no longer wanted to fight the battle of mixed emotions that I was dealing with. I couldn't do it alone anymore. After my cry out to my Heavenly Father, the dark cloud lifted off of me.

> *How could I love someone if I didn't love myself?*
> *How could I like someone if I didn't know who I was?*

I remember saying to God, *"I don't know who I am. Why couldn't I be a Daddy's Girl?"* That's when God showed me that **HE** is my Father…my **Heavenly Father**. He loves and protects me, even when I shy away from Him. The situations I dealt with, I had to go through for Him to deliver me so that **HE** would get the glory.

**I am enough. Once I realized whose I am,
it was then that I became complete.**

Listen: I have "been there, done that." I know what it's like to feel as if your heart has been ripped out of your chest. I know the pain you felt when 'he' left after verbally or physically abusing you. What I **ALSO** know is that when you get tired of being tired, your mindset will shift, allowing for a change to happen in your life. A lot of times, we teach people how to treat us. What we allow someone to say or do to us is in our control. Often, we choose to ignore the red, flapping flags because we look at only what we want to see.

I'm in my season. I'm worth the wait because I now know who I am. I am enough and worthy to be someone's queen. God delivered me from a toxic relationship (more like a "situation-ship" is what I like to call it). My healing didn't come from getting on the phone with friends or listening to man's advice. My healing came from me seeking out God and *FINDING* Him. Now, everyone has their own way of coping with things. Connecting with God was **my** way. I had to prepare myself to handle what God was about to do in my life. I endured a season when people I used to talk to daily then turned into talking weeks and then months later. I had to accept that I had asked God to take over. When I gave all my weary nights to Him, there were some lonely nights—and I mean that in a good way.

****

Dear Broken Woman,

As you flawlessly appear in the mirror while finishing the last touches of your makeup, know it will only last for a few hours. See, you're trying to cover up a pain that is deep within. I'm here to tell you that you wear it well. I didn't see the scars or the scratched surface before you applied your makeup but want to be there when you are removing it. I'm only here to tell you that you are enough and worthy to be praised. I know you're not asking for much. Love is, after all, supposed to be free, right? It gets costly when we end up with the wrong person or in the wrong situation. Sometimes, it can be a deadly price that's paid. It's okay to have mixed emotions, but only for a little while. Don't stay stuck. Don't allow your brokenness to lead you onto the path of vulnerability. I want you to know that you can stop applying the makeup to cover up. Love starts within, so love yourself first. Start investing in yourself physically, mentally, and spiritually. It's time to erase the shame and no longer allow the past to define who you are nor whom God is allowing you to become. It's your time to let God turn your mess into a masterpiece!

Signed,

A Healed, Equipped, and Restored Woman

NAKISHA D. BLACKWELL

Nakisha D. Blackwell is a Mother, Entrepreneur, Speaker and Co-Author. She is the CEO & Founder of KYW 'Know Your Worth' Online Boutique and Co-Author of *H.E.R Extreme Makeover: Reflections of Healing, Equipping, and Restoring Messes to Masterpieces*.

Email: kywboutique@gmail.com
Facebook: @Nakisha Blackwell
Facebook Business: @KYW Boutique
Instagram: @kyw_boutique
On the Web: www.kywboutique.com

Tschanna Taylor

Cheryl Menifee

"In life, we must prepare for the greater while we become acquainted with our own self-awareness, which becomes the benefactor of our birthright."
~ Cheryl Menifee ~

Dedication

My family has had to endure the transitions of my life and have done so without argument. I am grateful to them for standing as my strength with God as the center. There is nothing I can do without them both. I dedicate this story to them.

Why Not Me?

Let me start by saying this: I have struggled while writing this chapter. I didn't want to seem like a victim. I don't want to be pitied. I am not a perfect angel. In light of that, I had to stay in remembrance that everything we go through isn't for us. Instead, we are to pave a path to enlighten others — and we are to get free and **STAY** free. I am not going to tell my story traditionally (I haven't mastered that yet). Instead, I choose to tell my story conversationally. So, here we go!

For most of my life, I have had to console others about what I have come to represent in this life. I am done with that. My journey to "stand" started long before this time, but it is at *THIS* moment, I will answer the question:

WHY NOT ME?

I have been marked as the "nice girl" — the one who has never gone through anything simply because I can still laugh and enjoy life, even though I have faced many adversities. Those adversities included self-defeating patterns such as promiscuity, allowance of abuse (both mental and physical), putting others before me, and many other stagnating behaviors. Overcoming the dimming of my light for others was my hardest test. It took me many years before I put my foot down and pushed back on the opposition I built being "Superwoman."

How in the world did I build opposition against myself, you wonder? Well, I'm glad you asked!

I have always had a "knowing" about what my contribution to this world would be. With that "knowing," I walked in confidence. It wasn't an arrogant form of confidence that would shut others out or put them down; rather, it was the exact opposite—to build others up. My understanding of that contribution without direction assisted in a lack of boundaries that had me thinking I was a limitless source of energy. With my message, I attracted plenty of people willing to add me to their personal budget. I was added to their emotional budget, financial budget, spiritual budget…you name it. If it meant they could build themselves up from whatever superpower I was presenting that day, they made the "investment."

I didn't think twice, either. I gave it my all. I was a *Resolution Strategist* on steroids! If you were on a mountaintop and your shoe dropped 500,000 feet, you could depend on me to retrieve your shoe so that you could have a pleasant walk back down the mountain. Years of these patterns put me in an elite group: the "Can-Doers." I was gifted with an extra dose of optimism with a quick return of positive results. I am pretty sure there is a t-shirt floating around with my face on it that's titled **"The Woman Who Could Do It All!"**

With all of that going on for me, you would think that everywhere I went, they would roll out the red carpet. Nope! I am sorry to inform you that never happened. What **DID** happen was that I created enemies with the very people I was assisting! I went from being the "good girl" to the "girl who thought she was all that" (among many other wonderful names I will not list in this chapter). A special type of person will not like a single thing about you, be your "best friend," and take everything you have to offer at the time if you let them (no, I'm not bitter; it's a fact). They will not stop accessing you unless you close the door. Forget just closing it: **SLAM** it shut!

I **KNOW** what's going through your mind right now. *YOU* would *NEVER* let something that obvious happen to you, right?

Well, I have spoken those very words, so I ain't mad at you. I believed I was doing what was right and kept right on going. Can you believe it? I kept right on going!!! In my mind, I had decided that all I had to contend with were the side-eyes, snide remarks, and subtle negative energy. As a child of God, I could withstand anything!

You and I both know that overexposure to those elements was nothing more than a slow-burning recipe for disaster. I found out later that those great feats were among the list of main ingredients as to why I would begin to resent my strength. Oh, yes: I, Cheryl Denise, went through a period of resenting my own strength. I was so fed up with all the kickback from being there for other people, and I chose to take a time-out from my super duties. I wanted all who had made up their mind that any blessing I received should have been theirs, to stand up and move forward. I welcomed them to walk ahead of me and show me their leading abilities, instead of pushing me forward while throwing daggers and rocks and then hiding their hands. After all, they would not accept full responsibility if I was present.

This only proved to ignite the battle. People were so accustomed to me being a rock for them that they were angry that I was shielding myself. No matter how sincerely or in-depth I tried to explain my circumstances, the response — verbal and unspoken — was *"What about me?"* Their anger turned to action, more verbal attacks, inciting others to join them in their tirade, ignoring my children, and even criticizing my character. That was a turning point I could not ignore.

I was thrust into change. The resentment internally and the battle externally were depleting my energy. I slowly went into seclusion. As an introvert, being alone was not abnormal. This time, however, it was to save myself from the mess I had made **AND** become. My isolation set the stage for my restoration.

For my healing, equipping, and restoration, I took a spiritual, mental, and physical time-out. I desired to heal **H.E.R.** I was blessed to be able to remove myself from civilization and heal myself starting on the inside. For one full year, I did not connect with anyone I didn't have to. I immersed myself in research on healing, and I prayed. I relinked myself to my original promise. I accepted my imperfections as my own. I affirmed within that life was about learning the things I did not know to help supply me on my unique journey. I forgave others for being who they were so that I could get on with the business of being who I am.

What I have learned along the way is invaluable. I have learned:

- I am not God, and I am not without Him.
- There is no greater love than the one you can show yourself.
- How you love yourself creates boundaries for others naturally, so you must know who you are and what you want. Anything else sends a mixed message.
- None of us are without fault.
- We must tap into our own growth potential and live a life that is reflective of who we are meant to be.
- Others are not responsible for giving you anything; they are giving you exactly what they mean for you to have.
- Others will rarely see you because they are still learning to see themselves.
- Pressure does bring pain. It also produces.
- Separation isn't punishment; it's an educational segment of your life.
- We are subject to life, which has peaks and valleys — all of which is to grow us.
- Love is universal; however, how we are taught to love and how we execute love may vary.
- When someone has not learned to trust what God has given them, they will do anything to keep others in a position to serve their void.
- Most people are protecting themselves from the unknown — things that will not necessarily happen as they envision or presume they will.
- I can show up anywhere and "be." It's merely a choice.
- **I GOT THIS!**

There were times I didn't think I would be able to build close, personal relationships again. To have enmeshed myself in such unhealthy associations injured me. It also set itself as a catapult for my freedom. Despite the whispers of the shadows that faintly signified I didn't deserve to live a life of favor or how I wouldn't make it without them, I survived! I am still loving, giving, and growing—just as planned. I almost traded my peace for a life of enslavement. I even asked myself, *"Why do I have to be the one loving and giving?"* After my discovery season, I now ask, **"Why not me?"**

I walked in a subtle "knowing" that seemed secretive to some but simple to me. My confidence was predicated on the understanding that imperfection was my freedom—that because of this, I had the room to grow and become. While people were readily searching for their *"Why?"*, I was searching, too. It was much later when I realized my search wasn't necessarily for the *"Why?"* but the **"HOW?"** Asking questions for the wrong answers gave me many trials, tribulations, celebrations, and obliviousness. It was during the wrong search when I came to realize the importance of reciprocation in love, in sharing, and in life. It was essential to have a basic understanding of how to move from exhausting my life resource bank on others, to regaining focus on becoming the woman I already knew I was meant to be.

The wall of stagnation, competition, lies, deceit projection, gas lighting, conditioning, you name it abuse and dysfunction in any form has the production of fruit that has a great potential to damn our very walk. I sat in the presence of nothing but opposition. Many of our stories have sprinkles of these unhealthy characteristics floating around us or running through us. If we are real with ourselves, we know that our beginnings—no matter how loving the intent—has blinded us to the ways of the world and how the lack of preparedness has had us in the throes of what we will someday have to face, fight, and overcome.

I was never afraid to face obstacles. As noble and courageous as this may make me sound, I, too, had to face the music of some life choices that made me cry many days. With that, it also allowed me the opportunity of choice to recalibrate and grow. There is a pathology we all have, and to some, it has put us in a never-ending battle to…

Become what others think.

Become who we think we should be.

Become who God has already ordained us to be.

Wherever you find yourself in this walk, it is imperative you know that all is not lost. The necessary tools we do not or did not have for steady forward motion have to be added as we navigate every stumbling block to victory.

My personal life passage included emotional abuse, verbal abuse, physical abuse, vices, self-denial, perceived delayed success, people distractions, promiscuity, financial strain, physical health issues, depletion, and much more. For a long time, I would search diligently for the answers—especially when I hit the 35-year-old marker. I had begun to see the fruits of my own labor, and I panicked…**I PANICKED!** My panic clouded me for quite some time.

I couldn't believe the time I had lost in the promotion of others and the neglect of myself. I felt as though God trusted me with a lot early in my life, and I had taken every turn to demote the "knowing" of my own truth. Even though I had faith and knew what He had promised me, I still played the role of a fool to my purpose. Yes, I truly did. I am not ashamed; not one bit. In fact, I am sure many have walked this very walk. We must not lose sight of the fact that we had to start somewhere. Work with what you have! Life has a dynamic way of marrying your woes to your victory. It will not be unblemished but perfectly grounded in the faith of trusting there is more.

Fortunately, my story — **and yours** — is still being written. For that, I am thankful.

CHERYL MENIFEE

Cheryl Menifee, Emergent of an Esteemed Lifestyle, is an Author, Speaker, Magazine Editor, Event Facilitator, and budding entrepreneur.

She is a writing collaborator on *She Wouldn't Let Me Fall: 100 Stories of Faith, Forgiveness & Friendship* and *H.E.R. Extreme Makeover: Reflections of Healing, Equipping, and Restoring Messes into Masterpieces.*

In 2017, Cheryl established Esteemed Lifestyle as a business that focuses on the advancement of women who are establishing new or dormant ideas and passions through motivational practices, goal planning, accountability, and exposure using live or documented interviews.

"Your Vision; Her Support; Your Success" with "Excellence Void of the Illusion of Perfection"

Facebook: www.facebook.com/CherylMenifee
Instagram: www.instagram.com/CherylMenifee
Twitter: @cherylmenifee

Alisa J. Green

"God has a funny way of sitting us down, even if it means we have to be a part of a breakdown.
~ Anonymous ~

Dedication

I dedicate this story to all the women I know and love who struggle with self-limiting beliefs, self-doubt, self-love, and self-worth. It is my desire that after you read my story, you will find the courage to stand up, show up, and share your story to help other women heal.

My Mess and Masterpiece Through Love, Loss, and Business

Most of the time, when people ask me to introduce myself, I am hesitant to describe who I am. I believe that at one time, it used to be the part of me that I denied.

Who am I? I am a human being who's made plenty of mistakes in the past. Those same mistakes have shaped me. I have judged myself on occasion and held myself hostage to things I had no business holding myself hostage to. I'm a lover, a light, and a woman with a beautiful heart. I'm a lifelong learner, a healer, a rose, and a walking love letter. I am goodness. I love the sun and the moon. I am a loyal friend, sister, and daughter. I'm a comedian at times and a fire-starter. I'm a realist, and sometimes, I'm a crybaby. I'm a wine-lover, good listener, and a city girl with southern roots. I am a heartbeat and drum roll at the same time. I'm a daddy's girl. I am God's child.

My name is Alisa J. Green, and I am a light, igniting self-awareness.

I've been in business for quite some time. I was in business as a partner with my fiancé ten years ago, and that left me questioning: *Was this my dream or his?*

I moved on from there (not by choice) and started another business centered around my passion with a close friend. That venture lasted for a while. I had a fantastic time, but it was a learning experience, too. Although I was able to use my creativity, it also took up a lot of my time and energy. I was dealing with people who weren't as passionate as my partner and I were, so we closed the business.

My journey has been quite interesting and filled with lessons about love, loss, and business. The experiences were all intertwined somehow, but I couldn't see it that way when it was happening.

So, here I am in business again. This time—unlike before—I am fully-engaged, committed, and passionate about who I serve, my purpose, and my mission. This time, I clearly see that I should be focusing on loving myself (self-care) and the love for true sisterhood.

In 2011, I started "Coaching from the Inside Out." Before then, I had been on a journey for a few years, trying to figure out exactly what it was that I was supposed to be doing after suffering a tragic loss in my family.

When I think about it now, the losses are what made me begin to question everything and everyone. They left me feeling unsure, unstable, and alone. Those feelings lingered around for a while until I started to do some soul-searching.

I stepped outside of my comfort zone by connecting with women who were different from me. I held conversations with various people about passion and purpose. Those conversations turned into manifestations because a lot of things began to change with me. I experienced a reawakening after "sleepwalking" for so long. I believe there are messages in every conversation we have with other people; it's just a matter of listening carefully—and having a certain level of discernment.

So, I started meeting new people, visiting new places, and doing those things I put off while I was suffering through my loss. I connected with a coach who literally saved my life. She woke me up with compelling questions and held me accountable for the things I said I wanted and was going to do. She helped me get clear with my goals and helped me gain the confidence I needed to move forward—and I did!

Still, something didn't feel right. I was still suffering.

I knew if I was struggling to figure out what my purpose and passion were in life, then there had to be other women trying to figure theirs out, too. At that point, I knew I wanted to help women in my own way. Getting certified was just a stepping stone. I created the name of my business with the everyday woman in mind.

I believe that everything starts from the inside out. That's what is essential for us—as women—to remember. I thought that the coaching part of my journey in business was going to be a breeze, and I did my best to grow through it; however, I experienced a lot of resistance and made a lot of mistakes during my first few years in business. Those mistakes came from me overthinking and making myself feel like I needed to learn and do everything all at once. That was a disaster because it then turned into procrastination, leading to a feeling of disconnect from it all. It was time to change the dynamics of the journey.

I began to see things in a whole different light. I started reading more personal growth and development books. Doing so helped me take a closer look at my life in order to reflect, reassess, and recharge.

It became evident that if I wanted to help others, I had to support myself. It didn't feel right to extend my hand to help lift others while I was in pain myself. The journey was going to be more work than I could ever imagine. It was going to take a huge shift. I had to change my mindset and habits. While strategizing on how to move forward, I connected with others, doing things that I thought I should have already been doing in my business.

I was lost and experiencing traumatic loss repeatedly. It was in this shift that I decided it was time to heal myself so that I could help others heal. I knew that if I didn't change the things I needed to change, then everything would remain the same. I began to make some of the most significant investments in myself because I knew that if I didn't, I was going to continue to be all over the place. This whole situation was a hot mess!

I was overspending, overindulging in learning, and overthinking every move I wanted to make. The result was not making any moves at all. I was literally stuck! I isolated myself and made myself believe that I could recreate my experience all by myself over and over again until I forced myself to be still. What I needed to do was focus on healing. I think a lot of us miss the mark when we put ourselves last on our own list and still wind up in therapy after stressing out, burning out, and breaking down. It could be prevented if we choose ourselves first.

I dealt with a lot of pain. I found myself questioning my purpose and passion. I wanted to avoid all the losses that I had experienced in my life, but it was time to face all of those moments head-on.

If you are reading this chapter and you can relate, here is a question that requires your honest answer — and some tips to help you through:

Do you give yourself the proper self-care and nurturing needed to function on a daily basis consistently?

Heal. Equip. Restore. — Tips for you:

- **Check-in** — Find a space either at home or away from home where you can have some alone time to reflect and recharge. Understand the fundamentals and importance of self-care.
- **Take inventory** — Get your books, journals, candles, and everything else you need to de-stress.
- **Map out your plan** — You were put on this Earth to educate. Map out your next moves while your healing is in progress.
- **Commit** — You are a priority, so make yourself one and then spread your love and light.

- ❖ **Let it go** — It's time to release all of the things that no longer serve you in order to be able to get back to who God created you to be.

Bonus Affirmation:

I GIVE MYSELF PERMISSION TO SHINE. Today is full of opportunities. I am ready to shine and am so grateful to be a part of this thing called "life." I recognize that I have the power to change my life. I am worthy of unconditional love. I am God's child, and I am protected. I deserve endless abundance in all areas of my life. I am forever grateful for every twist and turn in my life because it gives me the opportunity to heal and grow.

ALISA J. GREEN

Alisa J. Green is a Certified Life Coach, Self-Care Specialist, Connecting Catalyst, and Host of Empower & GrowHER TV. She helps women empower, expand, and evolve themselves in their lives so that they can be more connected to their businesses through coaching programs and workshops. Alisa is the Creator of Coaching From the Inside Out, in which she also helps women get up close and personal by helping them create a better vision of **FREEDOM**.

Intenet: www.alisajgreen.com
Email: empowerandgrowher@gmail.com
Facebook: @coachinginsideout
Instagram: @iamalisajgreen
Twitter: @iamalisajgreen
LinkedIn: @alisajgreen

Sharice Rush

"It is great to minister to others, but there is a time called 'refill."
~ **Sharice Rush** ~

Dedication
I first dedicate my story to God, who is the Author and Creator of my life. To every spiritual leader who has contributed to my growth, I thank you. To my husband, children, parents, family, friends, and every reader: My prayer is that you will be encouraged by the many stories featured in this book.

Married in Ministry

I am a woman who, like many others, wears many hats: Mother, Wife, CEO, Mentor, Counselor, and Business Professional. In my church, I serve as a Minister, Youth Leader, Prayer Intercessor, and Community Outreach Leader. Following is my story of how being *"Married in Ministry"* can have its troubles. By the end, you will see there is **always** a solution with prayer, communication, and trust in God.

Being married in ministry comes with its challenges. Most often, people perceive only the glamorous side of marriage and ministry. Two people in love who are servants of God will *surely* have **minimal** relationship issues because both love the Lord. Many components make up marriage in a ministry that many people take for granted. I will discuss a few here: the balance of family and ministry, communication, and faith in God.

There was a time when all my husband and I did was serve in ministry. Every time there was a service or invitation to go out and minister, we were there. We loved the fact that God was always using us, and people's lives were transformed.

One thing we did not take into consideration was how fast our family grew the first two years of our marriage. Even though we love God, we also had the responsibility of raising our children. That is where the balance of family and ministry came in. For years, we spent more time in the church than with our children. The children were with us, but when you are raising them, they still need that bonding time. The Bible talks about home as our first ministry. It was easy to get caught up and not realize that our children were given to us to nurture and train them in the way they should go, not only spiritually but also naturally. The Bible says in 2 Peter 1:3 that God gives us all things that pertain to life and godliness.

Once the children got older, they were used to the activities of the church. Our children were growing up, and natural occurrences like peer pressure in school, hormonal changes, and worldly temptations began to rise in their lives. We have always been open to and for our children but for them, it was not easy to communicate certain things with us — such as peer pressure — when mom and dad were **always** at church. Things happened in our home that caused our house to be divided. Soon after, total chaos ensued. *How did we allow that to happen?* When the enemy comes in like a flood, he is out to steal, kill, and destroy.

One thing we learned was that we had to take time out and **create** family time to really talk about the things that were going on that caused division and hurt. We had to learn that it was okay to attend events that our children had at school and in the community. We had to make time to listen to and guide them in the way they should go.

Remember: Children can have mixed emotions about how parents are at church and how things are for them at home.

Communication is a vital part of marriage and ministry. Married couples must be able to communicate not only with God but also with their spouse. There was a time when chaos entered our home because of everyday life challenges. My husband and I stopped communicating with each other. We were not totally silent but spoke in passing and when we were in the church around others. The stress of work, bills, needs of the children, and requirements to be at church were consuming our time, leaving us incommunicative as a couple. I felt like when it came to us being a *married couple*, we were just two roommates in passing who shared the bills and had children.

Now, when it came to church, that was a little different because we were leaders in the same ministry. Things got to a point where we slept in separate rooms for years. It wasn't at all because we **hated** each other; we simply didn't carry on like a couple — other than when we were around other people. Soon, things started to really get rocky in our marriage, including various temptations such as alcohol addiction and adultery.

Communication is vital as well as communing with God. When you commune with God, He begins to show you things that need to be dealt with. Those things could be communication with your spouse, how to pray for your spouse, and how things as simple as spending time with them can show you what is really going on in each other's life.

Learn to recognize the tricks and plans of division from the enemy against marriage.

Lastly, faith in God is an essential element with being married in ministry. It is imperative that you have faith that the relationship is doable. Through the many challenges in life — whether it be family, ministry expectations, marriage, finances, or even tragedies — you must have faith that God will bring you out of every situation. Having faith in God is spending time alone with Him, as a family, and especially as a married couple. This will help keep hope in the promises of God. Some people profess to have faith, but when the rubber meets the road, they find they really don't trust and have faith that God can bring them out of certain circumstances. They forget to spend time with Him and that they need to continuously renew their mind with God's Word concerning every part of their lives.

It is great to minister to others, but there is a time called "refill." You can give out so much, but you need to be refilled to give *more*. This comes from spending time with God and building your faith in Him.

In conclusion, I have mentioned a few of my messes while being married in ministry. Through the many challenges my husband and I have faced, there were some main components that allowed us to make it through 19 years of marriage. Prayer, communication, taking time out for family, and faith in God helped our mess be changed to a continuous building of masterpieces.

One Bible passage that I have always kept with me during the personal challenges in my life is Philippians 1:6:

"I am convinced and confident of this very thing; that He who has begun a good work in you will perfect and complete it until the day of Jesus Christ."

A Prayer of Purpose:

Father God, I thank You for loving and creating me for Your great purpose. I thank You for never leaving me nor forsaking me through my many messes. I pray that You continue to perfect me until the coming of Your Son, Jesus Christ. Help me to be a better communicator with You and others. In Jesus' name, I pray. Amen.

~~~~~~~~~~

SHARICE RUSH

Facebook: @signerstouchofpaparazzi
Facebook: @sharicerush
Email: sharicerush@gmail.com

Conclusion

We all have experienced peaks and valleys as we journey through life. Sometimes, the valleys are self-inflicted. We make mistakes. We pay for every action in which we fail. Other times, challenges come to us as no fault of our own.

Personally, I know all too well how these moments can stop us in our tracks.

The takeaway I want you to grab from this book is that you've been called to a purpose that will be fulfilled — no matter what your "mess" looks like. Every experience from childhood to now is a part of the process that determines how you flow and move in your life. You cannot overcome life's challenges on your own. You need a realistic strategy, plan, or system of trusted loved ones and peers. Everyone's story matters. Your story of resilience, perseverance, and overcoming will not only help you realize your purpose but also inspire others to stand boldly in their truths.

If you have learned anything from this book, you will agree that our collective stories are no different than anyone else's. There are no "better stories" because they are all **OUR** stories! We live in a broken world where dreams shatter, drugs destroy, parents abuse, spouses cheat, pastors fail, children rebel, and death devastates. For some, it's a world in which there doesn't seem to be any hope for change.

This is not the end, my friend. The grace of God **always** has the last word to change our *mess* into a *masterpiece!*

Maybe you have read this book and saw through our experiences similar encounters within your own life. Perhaps you've even said to yourself, *"But they don't know what I have done or who I am!"* If those words are reverberating back and forth through your mind, don't you **dare** lose hope! These words are for you! The words shared on the pages of this book come from an R-rated place of transparency from women who have experienced mess in all areas of life to include health, wealth, spiritual, and business ventures.

Every day, I have to renew my mind and admit my faults or shortcomings, but I don't beat myself up for having them. I've been through too much to continually repeat cycles that no longer serve me.

There is some good news, though: **No matter how badly we've messed up, our mess is not measured by how well we have done or how "lovely" we are.** Our lovability is not based on our actions; it's based on the Master Designer, being our Creator and loving us as we are because of His Son. Whether we believe it or not, we are truly *His Masterpiece.*

Doesn't that make you breathe a sigh of relief?

I wish I were near you to extend to you a great, big hug. Living **unapologetically** and **authentically** means knowing that we can't mess "it" up and that we are masterpieces, no matter what we do or have done. It also means living in the truth that there is nothing we can do to make God love us any more or any less than He already does.

Take a deep breath, knowing that the Master Designer — in all of His sovereignty — is in control and has us on His mind all the time. Believe you are loved. Be at peace and free in your "mess"!

YOU ARE A MASTERPIECE!

About the Compiler

Tschanna M. Taylor, MBA is President and CEO of Tschanna Taylor Enterprises, LLC, a personal and professional consulting firm focused on helping storycrafters on a mission to redefine, reaffirm, and rebuild the stories of their lives.

Affectionately known as "The Purpose Engineer," Tschanna is a Speaker, Facilitator, Trainer, and Consultant with more than 25 years in business and the human resources corporate environment.

Tschanna has extensive experience and a diverse background in the areas of administration, leadership, church administration, authoring non-fiction books, publishing, marketing, branding, coaching, strategic development, professional development, personal development, event production, and training. She has also written various books and training programs.

Tschanna holds an Associate's Degree in Organizational Leadership; a B.S. in Business Administration; an M.B.A. in Human Resource Management; and a Graduate Certificate in Pastoral Counseling/Life Coaching. She is a five-time international best-selling author, contributing to numerous collaborative works.

Serving as an active member of the International Advisory Board for the Professional Woman Network in Louisville, Kentucky, she is also a Certified Life Coach in the areas of self-esteem, health and wellness, pre-marital and marital, and business coaching to name a few. She is a member of the Women Speakers Association, Dynamic Professional Women's Network, HIScoach Training Academy, Non-Fiction Author's Association, and American Association of Christian Counselors.

Set apart by her transparent delivery and transformative storytelling abilities, anyone can clearly see that Tschanna is resilient about helping others operate authentically and unapologetically in their God-given purpose.

For bookings or more information, email: info@tschannataylor.com or visit www.tschannataylor.com.

How to Use This Book

SMALL GROUP USE

Ideally, *H.E.R. Extreme Makeover: Reflections of Healing, Equipping and Restoring Messes into Masterpieces* can be used as a curriculum for discussion among a small group. In these groups, a facilitator gathers with up to ten other women to discuss the Reflection Questions following this section, and to hold each other accountable to take the steps necessary toward change.

Small groups can originate in your church, your Sisterhoods, or your women's networking organizations. You might even choose to gather informally with a few friends and neighbors to form a group. If you are not able to form a group, you can contact info@tschannataylor.com to see if there are groups already meeting in your area that you might be able to join. Feel free to join us in our private, free community, at https://www.facebook.com/groups/TTaylorIAMIMPORTANT/

INDIVIDUAL USE

Although a small group setting is the ideal way to grow with ***H.E.R. Extreme Makeover: Reflections of Healing, Equipping and Restoring Messes into Masterpieces,*** the book can also be used individually. After reading the Reflection Questions, write down your responses and take the steps necessary toward change. If you are able to find another woman to read through the book at the same time, you can encourage and empower one another!

Reflection Questions

1. When you find yourself in a difficult situation, what is your first response? Who do you turn to first?
2. Think of a time when you relied on your own understanding to solve a problem? What was the result? How did this impact you emotionally, spiritually, mentally, and/or financially?
3. How does pride raise its ugly head in your life?
4. When you look in the mirror, what do you see? List three adjectives of yourself that come to mind (e.g., kind-hearted, beautiful, driven, etc.).
5. Have you ever questioned God about why He allowed a difficult experience in your life? Be honest and record your thoughts or share with the group.
6. Do you struggle to trust people and find yourself being cynical or skeptical toward others? What caused you to arrive at this place?
7. How has hearing others' open and honest testimonies impacted and inspired your life? How can you pay it forward?
8. What are some ways Satan uses to distract you into messes? How do you overcome?
9. Are you angry with someone in your life whom you feel or felt has let you down? What role can forgiveness play in helping you to heal from those hurt feelings?

10. As you read the chapters of the authors, what was your initial reaction to the authors' confessions and the sharing of their messy circumstances? Have you connected with any of them on social media to let them know what you thought about their stories?
11. Do you find it difficult to share your "mess" with others? Why or why not?
12. What are you hoping to be revealed to you after you have had an opportunity to work your way through this book?
13. In what ways do you find it hard to admit your messiness?
14. In what ways might you be hiding behind the mask you are wearing? Be honest here.
15. Why is it important to recognize our imposter-selves?
16. Have you ever had a moment of exposure that has led you into freedom? How did you get free? If you're not free, what steps will you take to be free?
17. What are the things in your life that make you want to run from God?
18. How does knowing that God seeks you out in your mess help when you really want to run?
19. In what ways do you hear God saying, "I will not let you go"?
20. Write down your special skills, talents, and gifts. What are you really good at?
21. Think back to the dreams you had as a child and write them down. Is it possible those dreams could still be in your heart today? Are you ready to move forward in God's way?

22. What giant fears may be in the way of you stepping out in faith and trusting God's plan for your life?
23. Describe a time when you procrastinated to complete a task rather than followed through. What were the results? List both positive and negative results. Be honest.
24. List two goals that you will take action on to help fuel your faith and help you begin to make a bold move towards your life.
25. What evidence have you seen in your life that clearly has transferred to other areas of your life (e.g., life, health, wealth, spiritual, and business)?
26. What small steps are you willing to take to improve your diet?
27. What motivates you to exercise?
28. What is causing you to not get eight hours of sleep daily?
29. Is living behind a mask working for you? If not, what will you do differently to remove the mask?
30. What obstacles block you in your relationships?

So, What's Next?

Did this book bless your life? If so, I encourage you to:

- Write a book review on Amazon, your blog, a retailer's site, or my website at www.tschannataylor.com.
- Share what you've learned with a friend and ask her to hold you accountable.
- Share your comments or testimony with me at www.tschannataylor.com or www.facebook.com/tschannataylor
- Give this book as a gift to friends, family, co-workers, and others.
- Talk to your women's ministry leaders or Sisterhood director about starting a group or book club, using this book as the topic of discussion.
- Invite me to speak at a women's retreat or conference.
- Start a discussion on your social media sites and tag me at:
  #tschannataylor
  #messtomasterpiece
  #iamhealedequippedandrestored
  #HERExtremeMakeover19
- Follow Tschanna Taylor on social media @TschannaTaylor and tell us what you like.

Tschanna Taylor
"Your Purpose Strategist"

Tschanna assists her clients in identifying what they truly want through her down-to-earth delivery. She takes a strategic-based approach to help purpose-driven achievers own and grow in their purpose. Through her teachings, she focuses on each client's unique talents, abilities and gifts, while educating them on the skills necessary for profitable success so they can redefine, reaffirm, and rebuild their lives.

Dates are limited. Book Tschanna Taylor today at www.tschannataylor.com.

Connect with Tschanna

Subscribe to her blog at www.tschannatylor.com, send her a note and read more at www.tschannatylor.com.

   @TschannaTaylor or m.me/tschannataylor

Join the FREE, private Facebook community, Queenality, at https://www.facebook.com/groups/TTaylorIAMIMPORTANT/

Books by Tschanna Taylor

- After the Affair: Moving Forward God's Way
- Promises for A Woman of Purpose – Devotional Journal
- Woman of Influence Journal
- H.E.R. Extreme Makeover: Reflections of Healing, Equipping, and Restoring Life's Messes Into Masterpieces
- "All In" Strategies of Life from an Ex-Poker Player – **Coming 2020**

~~~~~~~~~~

Collaborative Works

- Blooming Into Your Purpose: Out of the Ashes Into the Son
- Turbulence: A Practical Guide on How to Remain Resilient in the Midst of Every Storm
- Affirmations & Antidotes That Strengthen Me
- Being Woman: A Sacred Journey of Reconnecting to the Divine Truth of Who You Are
- The Professional Woman: Self-Esteem, Confidence & Empowerment
- I Am Healed Devotional Anthology
- The Purposed Woman 365-Day Devotional
- Borderline Fine: How to Find Time to Do It All…For Women by Women

www.ingramcontent.com/pod-product-compliance
Lightning Source LLC
Chambersburg PA
CBHW052140110526
44591CB00012B/1794